I0112266

Secular, Sacred, More Sacred

ICETE

Global Hub for Evangelical Theological Education

Langham

GLOBAL LIBRARY

There is not a square inch in the whole domain of our human existence
over which Christ, who is Sovereign over all,
does not cry,
"Mine!"

Abraham Kuyper

This book comes at the right time. The divide between the secular and the sacred, the world and the church, society and faith needs to be addressed. This tragic schism is part of the legacy of Enlightenment and Modernity. Religion and faith have been pushed into the private sphere and have disappeared from public life. Pious evangelicals have played along with the game, and with their flight from the world have often even deepened the gap between public and pious life. I was inspired by the ICETE 2018 Triennial Conference in Panama City on the "The Secular-Sacred Divide and Theological Education," and I am delighted that the fruit of that conference is now documented and accessible. If the divide between the secular and the sacred is to be overcome, it must begin with the education of the next generation of leaders. This book shows ways forward.

Bernhard Ott, PhD
Chairman of the European Council for Theological Education
Professor and Supervisor of Doctoral Research and Dissertations,
European School of Culture and Theology, Korntal Campus,
Columbia International University, South Carolina, USA

This book provides thought-provoking biblical foundations in the early chapters, followed by encouraging practical examples, and finishes with appealing insights for action in the final chapters. This carefully crafted series of writings from multiple perspectives, together with reflection and discussion questions at the end of each chapter, is ICETE's helpful, new resource for theological educators and seminary leaders around the world. The volume addresses the sacred-secular divide problems in seminaries and brings the conversation further on the strategic roles of seminaries in advancing Lausanne's biblical vision to bring the whole gospel to the whole world, by the whole church.

Sutrisna Harjanto, PhD
Principal,
Bandung Theological Seminary, Indonesia

One of the areas where clear contextualization work needs to be done by higher theological education institutions globally is in the area of the unfortunate divide between the so-called "sacred" and "secular" vocations in the evangelical community. Most evangelical believers consider that they have a holy calling and a sacred ministry from God only when they work in church or church-related contexts. If they are involved in pastoral ministry, preaching and some kind of evangelistic activity, they say that they are "called" and their work is "spiritual." Whereas, if someone is working outside of the church context, his or her job is not considered either a calling or spiritual. In *Secular, Sacred, More Sacred*, Brooking, Branch and Villanueva tackle this issue head-on and present four calls made by different voices, both from the church context and the so-called secular context, to bridge this divide. This book is a lens that gives a new perspective to God's people, in whatever vocation they are in, to see their job as a God-given calling to partake in the expansion of his kingdom throughout the world. The unbiblical dichotomy between the secular and sacred vocation must be discouraged. This book shouts loud and clear that God has called us to be salt and light both in the church and in the market place. I highly recommend those in higher theological education and in the evangelical community to listen to and echo these clear voices and urgent calls to bridge the divide between the secular and sacred.

Frew Tamrat, PhD
Principal,
Evangelical Theological College, Addis Ababa, Ethiopia

Secular, Sacred, More Sacred

Four Calls to Bridge the Divide

General Editors

**Stuart Brooking, Paul Branch
and Federico G. Villanueva**

Series Editors

Riad Kassis
Michael A. Ortiz

ICETE

Global Hub for Evangelical Theological Education

Langham

GLOBAL LIBRARY

© 2021 International Council for Evangelical Theological Education

Published 2021 by Langham Global Library
An imprint of Langham Publishing
www.langhampublishing.org

Langham Publishing and its imprints are a ministry of Langham Partnership

Langham Partnership
PO Box 296, Carlisle, Cumbria, CA3 9WZ, UK
www.langham.org

ISBNs:
978-1-83973-435-9 Print
978-1-83973-441-0 ePub
978-1-83973-443-4 PDF

British Library Cataloguing-in-Publication Data
A catalogue record for this book is available from the British Library.

ISBN: 978-1-83973-435-9

Cover & Book Design: projectluz.com

Contents

Preface

This book is being edited and released during the COVID-19 pandemic. There is an all-pervasive sense to that reality around the world. The origins of the book predate this time of transition and so as editors we have sought to reflect both these contexts. The chapters are unchanged, but the reader will note that in our introduction, section introductions, study questions and postscript we have sought to take into account the new context and allow interpretation of the original writings within this changed environment.

At the time of editing it is impossible to guess just how disruptive the pandemic will be to the world, or what new realities will be embraced in the theological education space. We hope that the issues raised will be of benefit to seminaries around the world in whatever new political, economic and ministry context they find themselves.

The chapters of this book grew out of the ICETE 2018 Triennial Conference held in December that year in Panama City. The theme for the conference was "The Secular-Sacred Divide and Theological Education," and it drew several hundred attendees from all parts of the globe. The conference involved stimulating plenary sessions and numerous seminars. Just a small portion of the activity is captured in this volume.

We commend the work of these scholars and their various insights from the Scriptures, theology and education, and hope that it will provide a stimulus to process an integrated view of God's world within the seminaries. Their goal and ours is that the church and Christian people everywhere will be strengthened to live under the lordship of Jesus Christ in all their lives.

Stuart Brooking, Sydney
Paul Branch, Guatemala
Federico Villanueva, Manila

Introduction

Apologia

At the conclusion of the ICETE 2018 conference in Panama, Dr. David Baer presented his reflections aided by a representative listening group who had deliberated with him throughout the conference. His eloquent and insightful presentation left the attendees with many things to contemplate. The most significant issue he raised, for the conference itself and for the editors of this volume in particular, questioned the importance of the topic itself. Is the sacred-secular divide really an issue for the church?

To some attending the conference, the sacred-secular divide theme seemed a very 1990s kind of topic, one already addressed through a number of books and incorporated into the teaching of seminaries and church leaders. As editors, we have reflected upon both the important advances made in recent decades towards bridging the sacred-secular divide, as well as the distance yet to be covered as the church continues to address this important issue. In this preface, we offer a cumulative argument for the topic to remain in our Christian discussion and to continue as a part of our agenda, and not be merely ticked off the list of issues within our theological education enterprise. We hope thereby to demonstrate the pertinence of this new contribution which addresses the challenge of the sacred-secular divide from a fresh perspective and from a range of approaches. We hope this book issues a timely call to theological educators and the global church, to address this topic with renewed focus.

Our apologia covers the areas of theological reflection, societal analysis and observations of current theological education, especially in the Majority World.

Docetism

The idea in Christology that Christ is really divine and only appears to be human has analogues in many parts of Christian living. It has proved a lasting temptation in different expressions of the Christian faith in Christology proper, but also in a range of other parts of theology and in practical living. It underpins a tendency in some people to strive for a higher way and to denigrate the worldly pursuits of the majority. Its Neoplatonic routes are well mapped, and it results in a pious drift that so emphasizes the practice of the sacred, in whatever particularity, that it demonizes the secular as ungodly.

Just as with christological docetism, the sacred-secular dichotomy in living undermines a proper appreciation of the teaching of the Scriptures which values all the creation and emphasizes a new creation, not a disembodied spirit future.

Since the church has had to grapple with different forms of the sacred-secular divide over two millennia, it warrants an occasional reflection within theological education to ensure both curriculum and hidden curriculum are aligned to the biblical presentation of the integration of the sacred and the secular.

Materialism, Secularism and Globalization

While philosophical materialism is not new, acceptance of it in the West has taken a leap since the Enlightenment. For many, this mindset has become de rigueur. One driver of this growing hegemony is the process of secularization which has undermined a broader commitment to spiritual realities but has also influenced the way of faith for the faithful. A practical outworking of secularism within the church has been to compartmentalize people's experience of God so that it is more difficult to apply the life of faith outside specifically Christian environments. One conception of this problem is the sacred-secular divide. Proponents of this critique then seek to reinfuse all of life with spiritual value and encourage commitment to live intentionally for Christ in every part of one's life.

At a practical level in the 1970s and 1980s, within the more liturgically oriented churches, there was an attempt to incorporate laypeople into the work of ministry. A subsequent partial critique of that movement has been that it again emphasized the sacred space as the more legitimate area for all of God's people and thus de-emphasized the importance of their ministry within the workplace and wider life.

This secular materialism is a growing force around the world. Its origins in Western thought and culture have knock-on implications in the Majority World which is both being influenced by the West and following similar development paths to the West. In particular, urbanization brings people together in new living and workspaces who would ordinarily be separated geographically. Such intermingling can lead to a conscious re-examination of whatever faith commitment previously existed or the change in societal bonds can lead to a gradual drift away from faith. For Christians, this can mean that the cohesion of earlier experiences of faith no longer has its sustaining social context, which can lead to a reduction of integration and thus introduce the sacred-secular divide.

Take the example of the call centres of Bangalore. Many young people, good at English or some European language, work together. Castes are mixed, religions are mixed and even young men and women work together and socialize. Young Christian people suddenly earn multiples of their parents' income. They have "gadgets" and motorbikes and work strange hours. They know the weather in London, or New York, or Sydney, so they can relate to their customers! We have had more than one conversation with Christian leaders about this phenomenon. One theme in those conversations is the incapacity of the young people's pastors to help them navigate their new (relative) wealth and lifestyle with their Christian upbringing. Their family of origin's understandings and their "Sunday identity" are separated from their week-long experience. This is just one example of globalization impacting the Majority World's experience of the sacred-secular divide.

Curriculum "Lag" in the Majority World

One further reason will be given for the relevance of the topic of the ICETE 2018 conference and for the offerings in this book.

When attending conferences such as the ICETE triennials it is easy to assume the competence of the leading seminaries in the Majority World. The best speakers are on show. The best examples are given. We all rejoice that it is so. Those who have attended several ICETE triennials could attest to the growing competence of Majority World theological education just using that snapshot, but that is not the whole story.

When visiting the range of seminaries in the Majority World it becomes apparent that there is a great disparity in many aspects of the education on offer. While the influence of the Western curriculum is waning, the change is uneven. One explanation of the true and untrue aphorism about Africa that "Christianity is a mile wide and an inch deep" is that the borrowed Western curriculum has dominated theological education. A similar critique has been made in the Philippines, where the term "split-level Christianity" captures the same idea.

Where contextual realities are ignored, and the inherited models of the foreign missionary era are the standard, then something like the sacred-secular divide is in operation. Of course, it will look somewhat different from how it is expressed in the West, but it is an issue nonetheless.

We rejoice that there are so many encouragements for seminaries in the Majority World to become more contextually relevant. Indeed, the previous triennial, ICETE 2015, focused on the theme of researching context to change curriculum.[1] Nonetheless, there is still much work to be done, country by country, by local seminaries to further this process. Where the older forms of the Western curricula persist in the Majority World, they embed the seeds of the sacred-secular divide, to the detriment of the local churches.

Summary

For these reasons – a docetic view of life, the influence of secular materialism and the lag in revising the curricula of the Majority World – there remains value in this context to ask questions about the sacred-secular divide. We hope that the insights of the presenters at ICETE 2018, some of which are captured in this volume, might be a guide for reflection and response in the seminaries of the ICETE community and indeed more broadly.

We have arranged the chapters in four sections around the theme of "Calls." All of them are in some way addressed to the seminaries. Each section has

---

1. S. M. Brooking, ed., *Is It Working? Researching Context to Improve Curriculum: A Resource Book for Theological Schools*, ICETE Series (Carlisle: Langham Global Library, 2017 [and French and Spanish translations]).

its own introduction outlining the value of the chapters, so they won't be prefigured here.

- Section 1: A Call to Integration
- Section 2: A Call for Virtue
- Section 3: A Call to the Church
- Section 4: A Call from across the Divide

Each chapter ends with discussion questions with suggestions for use in different contexts. We imagine that some questions will be used for personal reflection by faculty members and seminary leaders. Others are more suited to group discussion and would make an ideal basis for short ongoing professional development at, say, weekly faculty meetings, or as part of a Professional Development day.

We hope you find value in this contribution to the topic of the sacred-secular divide, that it helps you and your seminary to move towards a more holistic integration of the faith for yourself and your students, and that it equips them as they minister in the church. We long for an equipping of God's leaders to minister to every aspect of their people's lives so that Christ is all in all.

Section 1

A Call to Integration

We open this book with two exegetical papers calling for an integration of life and a rejection of the sacred-secular divide.

Dr. Chris Wright presented at the opening plenary of ICETE 2018. He gave this scholarly and devotional study of Psalm 86. The psalmist David writes in a time of great personal crisis and prays his way to a position of trust. At the core of his request is to have an undivided heart (v. 11).

This psalm is not focused on the sacred-secular divide, but rather, as Wright draws out, David's desire for integrity in all of life, undercuts any such divide in life. Wright summarizes this insight:

> The psalmist wants integrity in the way he thinks. For we so often do indeed have divided hearts. We suffer from distracted attention. We have mixed motives. We struggle with conflicts of interest. We get into compromising relationships that split our loyalties. And we easily absorb that dichotomized worldview of the "sacred-secular divide" and compartmentalize our lives accordingly (see pg. 19).

Wright serves us well though this devotion. It anchors the whole enterprise of this book by confronting the sacred-secular divide through seeking after God. King David's prayerful appeal for his personal integrity is based on the solid foundation of the past actions and the character of God himself. This in itself is an important insight to begin the discussions of around our topic.

Dr. Shirley Ho's chapter comes from a seminar presentation focusing on aspects of the theology of the Book of Proverbs. The salvation history perspective of Wright's exposition of Psalm 86 is well balanced by the wisdom perspectives in the Proverbs.

At first blush, and according to some traditions within Proverbs commentary, the book is a secular production. In this tradition it is viewed alongside the wisdom literature of the Ancient Near East suggesting few revelatory components. The Act-Consequence concept magnifies the choice and action of individuals, which leaves little room for God in the book. The absence of the mythic or cultic elements of faith is also suggestive that the book is a secular construction of life.

Over against such an interpretation, Ho argues with others that there is a strong structural and thematic argument to be made for the sacred interpretation of the book. Understanding the role of Lady Wisdom in chapter 9 is the pinnacle of this argument and interprets both this world and cosmic realities through this lens.

Ho argues that there is no sacred-secular divide but rather a sacred-more sacred divide. This is in keeping with the lived reality of the ancient Israelite whose understanding of life and the cosmos is illustrated in the temple structure which contains the holy place and the most holy place. She suggests that the journey language of the book provides an indication of movement from the sacred to the more sacred, reinforcing the basic premise that there is no sacred/secular divide in the book at all, but an integrated sacred space of life which has more sacred elements.

Ho's seminar on Proverbs was the first in a two-part presentation. Dr. Lily Chua builds on the categories derived from Ho's work and applies these to theological education. Chua's seminar follows immediately as chapter 3, and begins section 2 which looks directly at the issues for theological education of the sacred-secular divide.

1

Integrating Truths
Psalm 86

Christopher J. H. Wright

Psalm 86 is a very balanced psalm: it begins and ends in trouble! But it finds integration at its centre. It is balanced also in the way it is structured, in a pattern of concentric circles. This is a form of extended chiastic arrangement, in which certain key points in the first half of the psalm lead into a central point, and then occur again in reverse order in the second half. This pattern looks like A-B-C-D-C-B-A. It is not rigid or exact, but the pattern can be seen.

The application to our theme of the sacred-secular divide will become apparent as we move through the psalm. It illustrates and calls us to the biblical view of integration. In this case, it integrates the truth with belief and life.

Let's begin with the outer edges of the psalm. There we find a person very much struggling with his troubles.

A Person in Trouble (vv. 1–7, 14–17)

Verses 1–7 spell it out. Here is somebody who is "poor and needy," who cries for "mercy," who is "in distress."

Then verses 14–17 bring it all back round again. He is threatened by "arrogant foes" and "ruthless people." He feels in real danger. He needs God to step in and save him. He cries for mercy again and pleads with God to help

Psalm 86
¹Hear me, LORD, and answer me,
for I am poor and needy.
²Guard my life, for I am faithful to you;
save **your servant** who trusts in you.

You are my God; ³have **mercy** on me, Lord,
for I call to you all day long.

⁴Bring joy to your **servant**, Lord,
for I put my trust in you.

⁵**You, Lord**, are forgiving and good,
abounding in love to all who call to you.

⁶Hear my prayer, LORD;
listen to my cry for **mercy**.
⁷When I am in distress, I call to you,
because you answer me.

⁸Among the gods there is **none like you**, Lord;

no **deeds** can compare with yours.

⁹All the nations you have made
will come and worship before you, Lord;
they will bring glory to your name.

¹⁰For you are great and do marvelous **deeds**;

you alone are God.

¹¹Teach me your way, LORD,
that I may rely on your faithfulness;
give me an undivided heart,
that I may fear your name.
¹²I will praise you, Lord my God, with all my heart;
I will glorify your name forever.
¹³For great is your love toward me;
you have delivered me from the depths,
from the realm of the dead.
¹³Arrogant foes are attacking me, O God;
ruthless people are trying to kill me—
they have no regard for you.

¹⁵**But you, Lord**, are a compassionate and gracious God,
slow to anger, **abounding in love** and faithfulness.

¹⁶Turn to me and have **mercy** on me;

show your strength on behalf of your **servant**;
save me, because **I serve** you
just as my mother did.

¹⁷Give me a sign of your goodness,
that my enemies may see it and be put to shame,
for you, LORD, have helped me and comforted me.

and comfort him. This is the reality on the outer edge of the psalm, at the beginning and end, the outer circle. The NIV reads:

> Hear me, LORD, and answer me,
>> for I am poor and needy.
> Guard my life, for I am faithful to you;
>> save your servant who trusts in you.
> You are my God; have mercy on me, Lord,
>> for I call to you all day long.
> Bring joy to your servant, Lord,
>> for I put my trust in you.
>
> You, Lord, are forgiving and good,
>> abounding in love to all who call to you.
> Hear my prayer, LORD;
>> listen to my cry for mercy.
> When I am in distress, I call to you,
>> because you answer me.
>
> . . .
>
> Arrogant foes are attacking me, O God;
>> ruthless people are trying to kill me –
>> they have no regard for you.
> But you, Lord, are a compassionate and gracious God,
>> slow to anger, abounding in love and faithfulness.
> Turn to me and have mercy on me;
>> show your strength on behalf of your servant;
> save me, because I serve you
>> just as my mother did.
> Give me a sign of your goodness,
>> that my enemies may see it and be put to shame,
>> for you, LORD, have helped me and comforted me.

Here then is somebody under severe stress. He feels vulnerable, in danger and very weak. There is a pressing need for God's help. And that is surely the reality for so many of the Lord's people in the world today. We may know what the psalmist is talking about in our own personal experience. And we certainly know what believers are going through in many countries, under persecution, discrimination, threats and even martyrdom. Many of us in the ICETE family come from such regions and wrestle with how to go on being faithful to our Lord and our calling in such circumstances. These words of the psalmist find loud echoes in our own hearts.

The psalmist here pours out his troubles in the midst of his worship (a good and healthy thing to do). Clearly that does not instantly *solve* the problems, since they are still there at the end of the psalm. But he balances those problems at the outer edges of his psalm with two very powerful perspectives. He puts these also near the beginning and the end of the psalm – just inside that outer circle of trouble. He uses matching words and phrases to give us these two inner circles. And so we move on to . . .

Two Perspectives He Can Trust
Himself in Relation to God: He Is God's Servant (vv. 2–4, 16)

He mentions this near the beginning and comes back to it near the end. Look at verses 2–4 and 16:

> Guard my life, for I am faithful to you;
>> save *your servant* who trusts in you.
> You are my God; have mercy on me, Lord,
>> for I call to you all day long.
> Bring joy to *your servant*, Lord,
>> for I put my trust in you . . .
>
> Turn to me and have mercy on me;
>> show your strength on behalf of *your servant*;
> save me, because *I serve you*
>> just as my mother did.

"This is not just anybody crying out to you, Lord. I am your servant, the son of your maidservant." He is saying, "Lord, my whole family and I are faithful, loyal, committed servants of God. I've been serving you all my life, just like my mother!"

I don't think this is being touted with any arrogant sense of *entitlement*. Rather it is an appeal based on the fact of a *relationship*. A human master would have some sense of obligation to one of his own servants, to care for that servant and protect him or her; after all, it was in his own financial interests to do so! How much more then should the covenant God of Israel take care of *his* servants? If I have been faithful to the Lord, surely I can trust God to keep his promise and be faithful to me. So twice the psalmist virtually challenges God to be true to his word: "I put my trust in you" (vv. 2 and 4). "Lord, I'm *trusting* you to deal with me as your faithful servant, trusting you to fulfil what that relationship calls for."

This, then, is an appeal to the covenant relationship at a personal level. The God who made great promises to his people Israel as a whole must surely keep those promises to this struggling Israelite. So he gets this perspective into place, close to the outer edge of his psalm. He remembers who *he* is, a servant of the living God who will not prove untrustworthy or impotent. He will trust in that relationship with God, his covenant Lord.

God in Relation to His People (vv. 5, 15)

Twice he starts a verse with a very emphatic "*You*, Lord, . . ." (vv. 5 and 15), creating another inner circle, getting closer to the centre:

> *You, Lord*, are forgiving and good,
>> abounding in love to all who call to you.

> But *you, Lord*, are a compassionate and gracious God,
>> slow to anger, abounding in love and faithfulness.

He has referred to himself as God's servant. But he realizes that what really matters is not who *he* is, but who *God* is, in his character and nature. So that is where he turns – twice.

Look at the list of what the psalmist says about God. You are

- Forgiving
- Good
- Abounding in love (twice)
- Compassionate
- Gracious
- Slow to anger
- Faithful

Don't you think he is feeling better already? Whatever he may say or claim about himself, this is what he knows about God. "*You*, Lord, will always be like this."

There is a beautiful ancient prayer in the Anglican Book of Common Prayer that goes back to Thomas Cranmer in 1548. It is said just before coming to the Lord's table in the Holy Communion. In contemporary English, we pray: "We do not presume to come to this your table, merciful Lord, trusting in our own righteousness, but in your manifold and great mercies. *We* are not worthy so much as to gather up the crumbs under your table. *But you* are the same Lord whose nature is always to have mercy."

That is exactly the perspective of Psalm 86. The psalmist knows the God he is praying to, and he reminds himself of all the things God affirms about himself in the Scriptures. His words clearly echo God's self-identification in Exodus 34:6–8. That adds even more confidence to his prayer. God can be trusted because this is the God he is. This is the covenant God whom Israel knows, both from God's self-revelation and from his acts on their behalf.

So, then, our psalmist has put his troubles at the outer edges of the psalm – at the beginning and the end. And then, inside that, he has placed these two perspectives: who he himself is as a servant of God, and who God is as the loving, good and faithful Yahweh God, the covenant God of Israel. With these two perspectives in place, he now comes to the central truth, the integrating hub of the whole psalm, in verses 8–10.

Three Central Truths about God (vv. 8–10)

These verses are clearly central, with seven verses before and seven verses following. And once again, our psalmist has arranged what he wants to say about God very carefully in a concentric pattern that leads our eye to the very heartbeat of the psalm in verse 9. This is the integrating centre that binds the whole psalm together around its core truths. We begin with the first and last lines.

God's Uniqueness (vv. 8, 10)

Among the gods there is *none like you*, Lord;

. . .

you alone are God.

This, of course, is the great affirmation of what we call Old Testament monotheism. Israel was surrounded by nations with many other gods. And this psalmist is surrounded by people who have no regard for the one true living God of Israel (v. 14). That may well be true for many of us as well. Like the psalmist, we live in a world running after many other gods and idols – whether the named gods of other religions, or the more subtle idolatries of our cultures (gods of mammon, greed, consumerism, security, militarism, sexual gratification, the narcissism of self-fulfilment, etc.). The sacred-secular divide is in itself the result of a kind of idolatry of secularism that pushes God and faith in God out of the public sphere into the realm of private belief and opinion. And these surrounding gods and those who are devoted to them can be hostile, intolerant and seductive, severely pressurizing Christians to accept and collude in their dichotomized worldview and retreat into our own little "sacred" realm.

But for this psalmist, the anchor of his soul, the foundation of his faith, his rock in the midst of his troubles, lies in knowing the living and true God. He knows the only God there is and he knows he is in a right relationship with this unique and universal God, of whom there is no other.

That was his confession and faith as an Old Testament Israelite. How much more do we need to drop our own anchor in the assurance of the uniqueness and universality of our Lord and Saviour Jesus Christ – of whom there is no other.

But the psalmist knows more. This unique God has a unique track record.

God's Past Record (vv. 8, 10)

> Among the gods there is none like you, Lord;
> no *deeds* can compare with yours.
>
> . . .
>
> For you are great and do marvellous *deeds*;
> you alone are God.

The psalmist does not only know who the LORD God of Israel *is*, he also knows what God has *done*. The "marvellous deeds" of God refer, of course, to the great epic narrative of God's past victories, and especially to the exodus and gift of the land. That was the story that shaped the identity, faith and mission of Israel.

The psalmist has his present troubles, but God has his past triumphs. So he can bring all his knowledge of *what God has done* in the past into *what he needs God to do* in the present. He knows the story he is in. And it is the story of the God of mighty acts of salvation and deliverance, the God of past promises gloriously fulfilled, the God of the history of his own people, Israel. That story is a mighty encouragement to his faith.

This is one reason (among many) why it is so important for God's people to know the story of the Bible: the whole great overarching narrative of God's mighty acts of salvation. For the Israelites, of course, this pointed them back to the exodus, while for us, it points us back to the cross and resurrection of our Lord Jesus Christ. Our God is our Redeemer. "What a mighty God we have!"

However, knowing the story he is in does not mean the psalmist is living in the past. For he knows where this story leads, and that brings him to his most central point. This God, unique as the only living God, and incomparable in the record of his past deeds, also has a plan and purpose for the future. The story of God is nothing less than the mission of God.

God's Future Mission (v. 9)

Here at the very centre (eight verses before and eight after), at the heartbeat of the psalm, we have an astonishing assertion about the future of the world, the goal of all human history:

> All the nations you have made
> > will come and worship before you, Lord;
> > they will bring glory to your name.

If our psalmist learned the character of God from Exodus, he knows the mission of God from Genesis. For this is a clear echo of God's promise to Abraham that through him and his descendants all nations on earth would come into the realm of God's blessing (Gen 12:1–3) – a rich and expansive concept with many dimensions.

And when they come into Abrahamic blessing, they will come to worship the God of Abraham. That is the great future that the Old Testament points towards. It is echoed in many other places too numerous to discuss here (though you might like to browse through some of these texts: 1 Kgs 8:41–43; Pss 22:27; 67; 87; Isa 19:19–25; 45:22–24; 52:10; Amos 9:11–12; Zech 2:11).

So then, in the midst of his own present troubles and suffering, the psalmist affirms that the future is as full of hope as the past is full of promise. For God is the God of promise and therefore of hope. This is the mission of God for the ultimate future for all nations on earth, and so one struggling Israelite (or Christian) can have faith in the midst of a very difficult present.

Those enemies (who are still there, v. 14) will either come to acknowledge and worship the God of Israel, or they will face God's judgment if they refuse. Either way, the psalmist can leave them for God to deal with, in salvation or judgment. The future is secure because the future belongs to God and the kingdom of God. And we echo that confidence when we sing with Paul (who was echoing Isa 45:23–24)

> that at the name of Jesus every knee should bow,
>> in heaven and on earth and under the earth,
> and every tongue acknowledge that Jesus Christ is Lord,
>> to the glory of God the Father.
> (Phil 2:10–11)

What, then, is our psalmist doing in these central verses?

He is affirming the great central truths of the faith of his whole people, in order to sustain his own wavering faith in the midst of his struggles, troubles and suffering. He is encouraging himself.

But not just with superficial mantras; not by bolstering his self-worth or self-image; not with clichés about positive thinking and going to his happy place. No. He puts himself firmly into that great arc of the biblical grand narrative. He inhabits the story of God's historical acts in the past (vv. 8 and 10), and God's ongoing mission towards the ultimate future (v. 9), and he recites the reassuring truths of God's revealed character (vv. 5 and 15).

Here is someone whose example we can and should follow. In the midst of his troubles and his need, he turns to God – but not with empty-headed emotion. This is the God he knows is the only God there is, the God who has acted mightily in the past to rescue and redeem his people, the God who will one day be acknowledged and worshipped by all humanity through all creation.

Psalm 86:8–10 is a marvellously condensed summary of core biblical faith, which we can affirm in the even fuller revelation of God we have through knowing our Lord Jesus Christ.

But our psalmist has not quite finished. We can see how he is faced with troubles that still surround him – there at the outer circle of the psalm. And we can see that he has encouraged his own faith by affirming the great truths of the faith of Israel – there at the very centre of the psalm. But what does he pray for himself in the light of all this? Verse 11 tells us.

Two Central Requests for Himself (v. 11)

The psalmist asks God for two things.

To Stay Teachable (v. 11a)

> Teach me your way, O LORD,
>> that I may walk in your truth.
>> (NRSV; I prefer this translation of the second line to the NIV's
>> "that I may rely on your faithfulness.")

The psalm is ascribed to David – a king, a leader, a man with a busy life, a man expected to teach others. Yet he prays, "Teach me your way, LORD." He wants to go on walking in humility, truth and integrity. So he needs to stay teachable by God.

The psalmist wants integrity in the way he lives: to be governed by God's own truthfulness – even in the midst of his troubles. For the fact is that trouble, pressure and crises can easily twist our sense of right and wrong. They can tempt us to justify plans and actions that ordinarily we would avoid, ways that are dishonest or untruthful, simply to save our own skin (or our institution). But the psalmist says, "No thanks. I want to go on being taught and directed by God. I want to walk in his truth. I want to maintain my integrity, even under pressure and threat."

Those of us who are teachers of others need to remain teachable by God.

To Stay Focused (v. 11b)

> Give me an undivided heart,
>> that I may fear your name.

The literal Hebrew is "unite my heart." Give me a single-minded commitment. Don't let me be divided this way and that.

The psalmist wants integrity in the way he thinks. For we so often do indeed have divided hearts. We suffer from distracted attention. We have mixed motives. We struggle with conflicts of interest. We get into compromising relationships that split our loyalties. And we easily absorb that dichotomized worldview of the "sacred-secular divide" and compartmentalize our lives accordingly.

How much we need *united hearts* – not just unity among ourselves, but unity at the core of our own world of vision, desires, intentions and goals. This must be a large part of what it means to "love the LORD your God with all your heart and with all your soul and with all your strength" (Deut 6:4–5). If there is only one whole single God, then I must love and serve him with the one whole single me.

And the psalmist clearly believes that only if God answers his two prayers in verse 11 will he be able to do what he most of all wants to do in verse 12:

> I will praise you, Lord my God, with all my heart;
> I will glorify your name for ever.

Conclusion

I don't know, of course, what verses 1 and 14 might mean for any of us, or for any of those we serve within the ICETE family around the world. But whatever specific circumstances those cries from the heart arouse in us, it is surely time to reclaim the great truths of verses 8–10, and verses 5 and 15, and to pray those key requests in verse 11.

We may still have to go back out to the edges of the psalm and acknowledge the troubles and trials we face. But we do so strengthened with the integrating bonds of our core biblical faith: knowing the God we serve, knowing the story we are in, and knowing the guaranteed future ahead. With such faith we can indeed ask and expect the Lord to give us "a sign of his goodness," along with his help and his comfort (v. 17).

Questions for Personal Reflection and Group Discussion

1. As you reflect upon your life and ministry, in what ways can you relate to the stress and vulnerability the psalmist feels, and to the pressing need he expresses for God's help?

2. What do the perspectives that the psalmist confesses about himself in relation to God and God in relation to his people (vv. 2–4, 16) mean to you as you reflect upon your own struggles and needs, and those that your theological institution faces?

3. Pause and pray for yourself, your colleagues, your students and your institution, adapting the psalmist's words to your situation.

4. Reflect on the three central truths about God that the psalmist confesses in verses 8–10, regarding his uniqueness, past record and future mission. In what ways do they help you understand the importance of your teaching, helping your students in their relationships with a world that is often shaped by forces that are idolatrous and opposed to God's people and purposes? How can you strengthen your students through these insights?

5. As you reflect on the psalmist's requests in verse 11 to stay teachable and focused, united in mind and heart, can you think of any way in which you have become distracted or disintegrated in your love and service to the Lord? If so, you may want to take this opportunity to pray and ask for unity of heart, using the psalmist's prayer in verse 11 or similar words.

2

Insights from Proverbs on the Sacred-Secular Divide

Shirley S. Ho

This essay focuses on the book of Proverbs as a resource for our corporate thinking about the sacred-secular divide. This chapter discusses how Proverbs scholars have argued for the secular overtones/undertones of Proverbs. Following this, in chapter 3, Lily Chua will provide three theoretical insights or frameworks from Proverbs that may be useful for further reflection on the theme of the sacred-secular divide.

Secularity in Proverbs

James A. Baldwin, a black American novelist and social activist, made the following statement about the importance of definitions: "The power of the white world is threatened whenever a black man refuses to accept the white world's definitions." Hence, in this first section, the goal is to settle on an *agreed* understanding and common ground of what is "secular" and what is "sacred."

Indeed, what is sacred? What is secular? What is the modern meaning of these categories, and what do these categories mean in Proverbs? As we talk about definitions, I bear in mind two caveats.

First, I am mindful of how these categories are used across different academic fields: philosophy, social sciences,[1] ritual studies, theology, and so on. Second, I am aware of the danger of anachronism. I do not want to impose modern concepts on an ancient text like Proverbs. Bearing these factors in mind, my goal is still to find a way to talk about this concept of sacred-secular.

A variety of expressions is used to refer to the basic categories called "secular" and "sacred."

For the "secular," the list includes what is natural, the created world, the neutral, mundane, humanistic, profane, common, practical, worldly, and so on. The category called "sacred" includes expressions such as the grace, the religious, spiritual, supranatural, mythic, immanent, divine, and so on. To be sure, these expressions cannot be understood to be strictly synonymous. In fact, they are not equally legitimate. However, the expressions overlap in meaning and are comparable as different designations of the basic terms of the "sacred-secular" differentiation.

With various terminologies in mind, many Proverbs commentators using modern critical approaches have understood the book of Proverbs as a collection of practical and mundane instructions, advice, and wise sayings for everyday living. It is oriented to teach readers how to live morally and wisely "right here and right now." Proverbs is said to be devoid of any of the religious and cultic ideology of ancient Israel. Proverbs is also known for its alleged deistic secular-moralistic program. Recent scholars are determined to locate the book of Proverbs in its post-exilic context reflecting the socio-geopolitical realities of the time, rather than reading it in moral abstraction which was common in earlier decades.[2]

Michael Fox, who wrote the Anchor Bible Commentary on Proverbs, says:

---

1. The decline of reference to the divine in the public space; the decline of attention paid to the divine in private life; the decline of "mythical," "enchanted" or "sacral" human thinking.

2. Christine Roy Yoder, *Wisdom as a Woman of Substance: A Socioeconomic Reading of Proverbs 1–9 and 31:10–31*, Beihefte zur Zeitschrift für die Alttestamentliche Wissenschaft (BZAW) 304 (Berlin/NewYork: Walter de Gruyter, 2001); Tova L. Forti, "The *Isha Zara* in Proverbs 1–9: Allegory and Allegorization," *Hebrew Studies* 48 (2007): 89–100; Claudia V. Camp, *Wisdom and the Feminine in the Book of Proverbs*, Bible and Literature Series 11 (Decatur, GA: Almond; Sheffield: JSOT Press, 1985).

The social setting of the book of Proverbs is open to dispute, but it is clearly a *secular work*. It makes no pretence to an origin in divine revelation or inspiration. God is never quoted or addressed. It never had a role in the ritual life of Israel, in neither temple nor synagogue. In fact, it never was, and still is not, a subject of deliberate study in the rabbinic academics. With the exception of a few passages, it treats everyday life, not the grand affairs of state, history, cult or law.[3]

There are at least three definitions of "secular" that scholars have attributed to Proverbs. They are the following:

"Secular" as Neutral Space: Proverbs as International Wisdom

Katharine Dell writes, Proverbs "with its close association with International Wisdom; the question was raised whether this followed a more ancient Near Eastern doctrine of God as creator and 'world-orderer' rather than a particularly Israelite one."[4] R. N. Whybray's main thesis is that the book "consists of an original lesson-book designed for use in scribal schools and [is]closely modelled on Egyptian prototypes, to which later writers added interpretative material with the intention of bringing its teaching more closely into conformity with Israelite religious beliefs."[5] According to G. E. Wright:

> The difficulty of the wisdom movement was that its theological base and interest were too narrowly fixed; and in this respect Proverbs remains near the pagan source of wisdom in which society and the Divine work in history played no role. In the canon of Scripture, Proverbs has the important function of supplying an explanation of the meaning of the law for individual life. But to survive as a living force in Judaism and Christianity the wisdom

---

3. Michael Fox, *Proverbs 1–9: A New Translation with Introduction and Commentary*, Anchor Bible 18A (New Haven: Yale University Press, 2009), 7.

4. Katharine J. Dell, *The Book of Proverbs in Social and Theological Contexts* (Cambridge: Cambridge University Press, 2006), 127.

5. Roger Norman Whybray, *Wisdom in Proverbs* (Naperville: Alec Allenson, 1965), 7.

movement has to undergo a more thorough acclimation to the doctrines of election and covenant.[6]

William McKane spends the first section of his Old Testament Library commentary – a total of more than 150 pages – discussing International Wisdom, including the literary forms of instruction and proverbs found in Egypt, Babylon and Assyria.[7]

Proverbs is compared not only with Mesopotamian wisdom, but also with Egyptian wisdom. Scholars have observed that there is a close association with the Egyptian wisdom text *Instruction of Amenemope*, which is suggested as a template for Proverbs 22:1–24:22.[8]

Proverbs	*Instruction of Amenemope*
(Prov 22:17–18): Incline your ear and hear my words, and apply your mind to my teaching; for it will be pleasant if you keep them within you, if all of them are ready on your lips.	(*Amenemope*, ch. 1): Give your ears, hear the sayings, Give your heart to understand them; It profits to put them in your heart, Woe to him who neglects them! Let them rest in the casket of your belly, May they be bolted in your heart;
(Prov 22:22): Do not rob the poor because they are poor, or crush the afflicted at the gate;	(*Amenemope*, ch. 2): Beware of robbing a wretch, Of attacking a cripple;
(Prov 22:24–25): Make no friends with those given to anger, and do not associate with hotheads, or you may learn their ways and entangle yourself in a snare.	(*Amenemope*, ch. 10): Don't force yourself to greet the heated man, For then you injure your own heart; Do not say "greetings" to him falsely, While there is terror in your belly.

---

6. G. Ernest Wright, *God Who Acts: Biblical Theology as Recital* (London: SCM Press, 1969), 104.

7. William McKane, *Proverbs: A New Approach*, Old Testament Library (Philadelphia: Westminster, 1970).

8. English Translation of Proverbs is taken from NRSV; Translation of *Instruction of Amenemope* is taken from *Context of Scriptures*, Vol. 1, eds. William Halo and K. Lawson Younger (Leiden: Brill, 1997), 116–118.

"Secular" as Human Autonomy

Proverbs scholars have also observed the strong humanism or humanistic element in the book. This is especially evident with the "act-consequence" axiom which permeates almost all the book of Proverbs. The "act-consequence" nexus means that "if you do this, the result is this; but if you act that way, you get that." The axiom suggests a mechanical and formulaic world-order principle, manoeuvred by human beings (wise or foolish) with corresponding consequences, without reference to the divine. George Ernest Wright says: "The material in the book of Proverbs in particular, remains near the pagan source of wisdom in which society and the divine work in history played no role."[9] Samuel Adams, in *Wisdom in Transition: Act and Consequence in Second Temple Instructions*, argues that there is development in wisdom thought from its early to later stages, from an earthly to an otherworldly focus. He locates Proverbs as early, hence it "focusses on present circumstances and *the immediate consequence of individual actions*."[10] The lack of interference by the divine made Derek Kidner say: "A hostile reader might go even further, and ask whether the real god and master in this book is not man himself, and the real goal prosperity."[11] Claus Westermann, however, reads the phenomenon positively when he writes, "That wisdom, a secular concept, should [occur in] both Testaments of the Bible is due to the fact that it is inherent in creation – more specifically, human creation. The Creator bestowed on the human being the capability of finding his own way through life and of understanding himself . . . of distinguishing between that which is good or evil, beneficial or destructive."[12]

"Secular" as Disenchantment/Demythologizing/Absence of Mythic Elements

The last definition is the lack of mythical traditions in the book, such as rituals, sacrifices and cultic worship. For these scholars, what is contained in Proverbs

---

9. Wright, *God Who Acts*, 67.

10. Samuel L. Adams, *Wisdom in Transition: Act and Consequence in Second Temple Instructions*, Supplements to the Journal for the Study of Judaism 125 (Leiden: Brill, 2008), 95.

11. Derek Kidner, *The Proverbs: An Introduction and Commentary*, Tyndale Old Testament Commentaries (London: Tyndale, 1964), 31.

12. Claus Westermann, *Roots of Wisdom: The Oldest Proverbs of Israel and Other Peoples* (Louisville, KY: Westminster John Knox, 1995), 1.

is practical and mundane. Tova Forti writes, "In my view, the *Isha Zara* [Strange Woman] speeches do not differ from other issues of everyday life dominating the book of Proverbs such as family ethos, parental teaching, domestic harmony, and social stability."[13] She cautions against an allegorical reading of the woman as "a metaphor, a symbol, allegory of foreign cult, Greek philosophy, and 'OTHER' in manifold directions." She continues, "At the outset, I shall state my primary contention, namely that the Strange Woman of Proverbs 1–9 (2:16–22; 5:1–23; 6:20–35; 7:1–27) ought to be identified as a mundane, seductive, adulterous, married woman who threatens the safeguarding of the family nucleus and stability of the social order."[14]

Three Insights from Proverbs on the Sacred-Secular Divide

Having established the supposed secular overtone of Proverbs and various conceptualizations, I shall now proceed to highlight three thematic and conceptual insights from Proverbs on the sacred and secular.

First Insight: Secular as Neutral Space – International Nature of Proverbs

The first insight draws from Zoltán S. Schwáb. The title of his book is *Toward an Interpretation of the Book of Proverbs: Selfishness and Secularity Reconsidered*.[15] Schwáb has subscribed to the first category of "secular" and defines secularity in Proverbs as a neutral space for all different backgrounds to come together. He argues that Proverbs adopts the common language of humanity. He agrees that Proverbs has universal concerns, dealing with timeless human problems and general observations about life. He maintains that "the universal nature of the book could encourage the ancient as well as the modern reader to be engaged in mutual, appreciative conversation with other cultures."[16] This understanding

---

13. Forti, "*Isha Zara* in Proverbs 1–9," 89.

14. Forti, 89.

15. Zoltán S. Schwáb, *Toward an Interpretation of the Book of Proverbs: Selfishness and Secularity Reconsidered*, Journal of Theological Interpretation Supplement series 7 (Winona Lake, IN: Eisenbrauns, 2013).

16. Schwáb, *Book of Proverbs*, 176.

of the secularity of Proverbs is undoubtedly supported by ancient Near Eastern texts which share similarities with the secular and mundane tones of Proverbs.

Next, he analyses Lady Wisdom in Proverbs 8. He discusses in turn whether Lady Wisdom should be understood as a Platonic idea, the aphorisms and sayings of the book, the Torah, a literary figure standing for divine/human wisdom, Yahweh himself, the world order, or a hypostasis of God. He concludes that he is not interested in the identity of Lady Wisdom but in her relationship with God. Accordingly, Lady Wisdom in Proverbs 8 is described in multifaceted ways: on the one hand, Lady Wisdom is Yahweh,[17] but on the other hand, she is differentiated from Yahweh. Schwáb argues that, functionally, "wisdom is a mediator who mediates the presence of Yahweh or more precisely displays the presence of Yahweh in the world. When one sees wisdom, one sees Yahweh, so to speak."[18]

He further develops his idea and maintains that "Proverbs 8 depicts wisdom in/through which human beings can experience God's presence. But speaking about God's presence, or about the 'things' through which God is present, requires a dialectic language of 'where God is, is not God.'"[19] According to Schwáb, in choosing wisdom in that secular neutral space, one is participating in the divine and sacred and imitating the divine or sacred. He writes: "If I am right that wisdom is about being with Yahweh and this comprises the background for the reading of the whole book of Proverbs, then we can hardly call this book or the world and behaviour which it is about, 'secular.' Quite the opposite. The thrust of the book seems to be to encourage the reader to experience Yahweh in the world. In this sense, it is more about the 'sanctification of the secular' world than about worldliness."[20]

Following Schwáb's reasoning, when one chooses wisdom, one participates in the sacred and divine, even in the secular space. By choosing wisdom, one is sanctifying the secular. I agree with Schwáb's thesis on how wisdom sanctifies the secular. However, the danger with this understanding when applied to

---

17. Life and death depend on relationship with her; she is the source of government; she loathes wickedness like Yahweh; like Yahweh she is more precious than silver and gold.

18. Schwáb, *Book of Proverbs*, 188.

19. Schwáb, 182.

20. Schwáb, 188–189.

the contemporary secular world is the risk of the bifurcation of the divine Person from the divine teachings/wisdom. How does someone know that by choosing wisdom, he or she is encountering the divine/sacred? Does the sign conveniently and accurately point to the signified? The problem with modern secularity is to take the wisdom and teachings of God without God himself. The divine Person is dissociated from the divine teaching, values, and wisdom, which are instead associated with human endeavour and human glory. This is so-called "cultural Christianity"[21] which is antithetical to Proverbs' worldview. I would argue that such a bifurcation between the sacred and the secular (in its modern sense) is alien to ancient Israelite thought.

Second Insight: From "Secular-Sacred Divide" to "Sacred-More Sacred Divide"

In this second insight, I discuss the secularity in Proverbs by combining the two definitions of secularity suggested by scholars above, that is, Secular as Human Autonomy and Disenchantment/Demythology.

Thin Spread of Divine Presence and Mythic Language in Proverbs

Derek Kidner observes: "When we open the Book of Proverbs at random and take samples of its wisdom, we may gain the impression that its religious content is thin and indefinite. Many of its maxims and theological assertions would transplant into non-Israelite, non-biblical soil, and we are tempted to ask whether anything as specific as a covenant-relationship with God is presupposed here."[22]

Here I would like to affirm the observation of the strong tone of human autonomy and disenchantment in Proverbs. Human autonomy, as already mentioned above, is seen in the pervasiveness of the "act-consequence nexus" in the various aphorisms. Also, there is indeed an explicit absence of rituals, miracles and cultic language in Proverbs. However, while affirming the substantial elements of human autonomy and the absence of rituals and

---

21. "Cultural Christians" refers to deists, pantheists, agnostics, atheists and anti-theists who are not Christians but adhere to Christian values and appreciate Christian culture. This kind of identification may be due to various factors, such as family background, personal experiences, and the social and cultural environment in which they grew up.
22. Kidner, *Proverbs*, 31.

miracles, such does not completely represent Proverbs. Also, Proverbs is unique (both in form and in content) in the Old Testament. It is noteworthy that there are passages that speak of Yahweh's intervention and mythic elements, but only if scholars probe deeper.

Throughout Proverbs, the sages identify God as YHWH, the God of Israel (eighty-seven times), while referring to God as *Elohim* only five times. In Proverbs 16:9; 19:21; 20:12; 30:5, God is depicted as creator, sovereign over human decisions, and arbiter of all things, more than as executor or enforcer of wisdom. The famous words of Proverbs 3:5–6 are a caution teaching human beings to "trust in the LORD with all your heart and lean not on your own understanding." In other words, when a wise person makes choices and decisions in life, they are done in, with and by trusting the Lord.

Moreover, there is the presence of mythic language in the description of wisdom as the "tree of life" (3:18). This is reminiscent of the tree of life in Genesis 2–3. In fact, connections may be made with the pursuit of immortality found in the *Epic of Gilgamesh*. This pursuit of immortality is to be connected with the language of "adding years" or "adding days" to your life in the pursuit of wisdom (3:2, 16; 4:10; 9:11; 10:27; 28:16). It is Yahweh who prolongs human life. How exactly does that happen? It is supplemented by the New Testament resurrection of the dead and with the *Epic of Gilgamesh* as an ancient conceptual background. Death is also described in mythic language suggesting the sage's insights of the other-worldly. Death and the description of Sheol as the netherworld are seen below (NRSV):

> Prov 1:12: like Sheol let us swallow them alive and whole, like those who go down to the Pit.

> Prov 27:20: Sheol and Abaddon are never satisfied, and human eyes are never satisfied.

> Prov 30:16: Sheol, the barren womb, the earth ever thirsty for water, and the fire that never says, "Enough."

In other words, Proverbs "may be called the *documents of Israel's humanism*, not in the sense of a rejection of the supernatural, or even as intending a concern chiefly with man's welfare, but because its general characteristic is the recognition of man's moral responsibility" (author's emphasis).[23]

Wisdom in the Cosmic World

Proverbs describes the creation of the cosmic world as built through wisdom. Moreover, it is not just the *building* of the world that is carried out through wisdom, but also the *filling* of the world.[24] Insofar as wisdom is the *mediator* of divine presence, the means by which human beings experience God's presence (Schwáb), the following texts speak of divine presence in/through the cosmic world. This concept is, however, different from animism or pantheism.

> The LORD by wisdom founded the earth;
>> by understanding he established the heavens;
> by his knowledge the deeps broke open,
>> and the clouds drop down the dew.
> (Prov 3:19–20 NRSV)

> By wisdom a house is built,
>> and by understanding it is established;
> by knowledge the rooms are filled
>> with all precious and pleasant riches.
> (Prov 24:3–4 NRSV)

What is more, wisdom is not only pre-existent (8:22–29), but also the law that governs human society:

> By me kings reign,
>> and rulers decree what is just;
> by me rulers rule,
>> and nobles, all who govern rightly.
> (Prov 8:15–16 NRSV)

---

23. O. S. Rankin, *Israel's Wisdom Literature: Its Bearing on Theology and the History of Religion* (Edinburgh: T&T Clark, 1964), 3.

24. Raymond C. van Leeuwen, in his chapter "Cosmos, Temple, House: Building and Wisdom in Mesopotamia and Israel," in *Wisdom Literature in Mesopotamia and Israel*, ed. Richard J. Clifford (Atlanta: SBL, 2007), 67–90. He argues that in the book of Proverbs, wisdom is also connected to building the cosmos.

Hence, the depiction of the cosmic world in Proverbs tells us that there is no space or realm considered to be without the presence of YHWH or without the mediator of the presence of YHWH. Just as the world was created and indwelt by wisdom, so divine presence permeates the world. The whole world is the dwelling place of wisdom. Hence, there is no space or realm in the world that is not a product of wisdom.

Also, if we understand the cosmic world as the model of Israel's tabernacle in Exodus 25–40 and temple in 1 Kings 1–11 such that the sanctuary is a microcosmic house mirroring the macrocosmic house of creation, and that both the cosmos and the temple are said to be "filled" with the divine glory, then the world of the book of Proverbs cannot escape the divine presence.

Considering all the details and information above, a careful study of Proverbs will show that there is no absence of divine presence/the sacred in Proverbs. However, it has to be admitted that there is only a *thin* or less manifestation of divine presence. The strong presence of human participation is inferred only when compared with the narratives found in the Pentateuch, Deuteronomistic History and the prophetic books which centre on God's great salvific acts, rituals and worship. Without such a comparison, it is hard to draw such a conclusion.

Thus, in order to explain the reduced, or fewer, manifestations of the sacred in Proverbs we need to recognize that in these books (Pentateuch, Prophets) divine engagement with humanity and the world is more direct. But in Proverbs, God works *in* and *through* human beings who are created in his image. N. T. Wright speaks of God as *dia-anthropic* (God *through* human beings). The strong language of human autonomy suggests human agency rather than an absence of the divine. This human agency is evidenced by the strong emphasis in Proverbs of "choosing" wisdom and the way of wisdom (Prov 4:13; 6:20; 16:16; 19:8; 22:1; 23:23). Put simply, "less" does not mean "absence." "Indirect" does not mean "absence." In theological terms, God's immanence is not manifested, but this does not mean God is absent in Proverbs.

Special Banquet with Lady Wisdom in Proverbs 9

Having affirmed the presence – albeit a thin presence – of the sacred in the worldview of Proverbs, I contend further that there is more to the presence of the divine in Proverbs. For this we need to look at Proverbs 9:1–6 NRSV:

Wisdom has built her house,
> she has hewn her seven pillars.
She has slaughtered her animals, she has mixed her wine,
> she has also set her table.
She has sent out her servant-girls, she calls
> from the highest places in the town,
"You that are simple, turn in here!"
> To those without sense she says,
"Come, eat of my bread
> and drink of the wine I have mixed.
Lay aside immaturity, and live,
> and walk in the way of insight."

This is a pivotal passage in Proverbs 1–9. After all, Proverbs 9 is the last chapter in that section. I shall say more about the structure of Proverbs under the third insight (last section). It describes Lady Wisdom in her palatial temple (9:1). She prepares a banquet with a slaughtered animal (9:2). This banquet includes meat, bread, and drink especially mixed by her (9:5). She has servant girls to invite sojourners and guests to live by walking in the way of wisdom (9:3). She possesses the character associated with God. Overall, this banquet is the realm where the divine presence is best manifested and most felt.

The portrayal of Lady Wisdom in Proverbs 9:1–6 is different from that in the early chapters, for there she was on the street calling people to choose wisdom. The wisdom of the pathway was Platonic and instructional, but in Proverbs 9:1–6 we have a *personal* encounter with Lady Wisdom at a grand banquet dining with Lady Wisdom herself. Hence, this banquet represents the most sacred encounter with the divine.

Degrees of Sacredness in Proverbs

So we see that a gradation of sacredness is operating in Proverbs. This gradation should redefine our "sacred-secular" categories. Based on Proverbs, I propose that the conceptual categories be redefined *from* "secular" and "sacred" *to* "sacred" and "more sacred" (see figure 2.1). The secular-sacred divide may be a *category mistake*, at least in Proverbs! What we see in Proverbs is a gradation or degree of sacredness represented from light grey to dark grey. Thus instead of

(1) the presence or absence of sacredness, or (2) the sacred sphere differentiated from the secular sphere, in figure 2.1, the dark grey represents the realm closer to the heart of the divine presence.

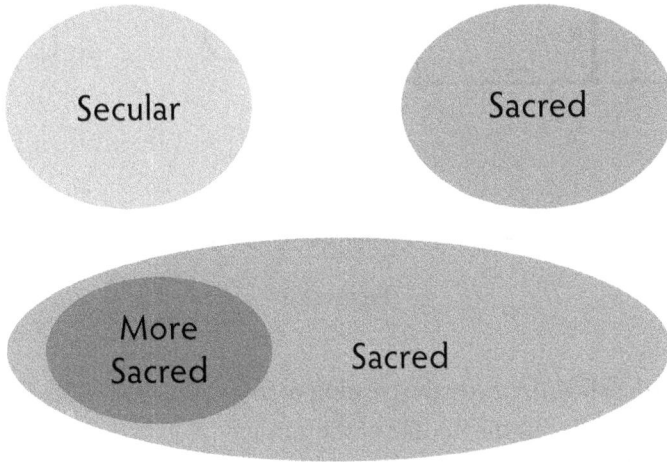

Figure 2.1

Degrees of Sacredness in Israelite Cognitive Lived Reality

In support of the above thesis is the fact that the gradation of sacredness is in accordance with the ancient Israelites' lived reality and cognitive worldview, not just with the literary world of the book of Proverbs. Israelites saw the world differently from modern people. From ancient Near Eastern sources we now know that the Old Testament and Jews conceived the cosmic world we live in as the dwelling place of the divine being, Yahweh. The whole world was the temple of God where God dwells. Just as the tabernacle was divided into a three-partite structure (outside tabernacle/Holy Place/Most Holy Place),[25] so with the cosmic world (visible world [where humans live]/visible heavens/invisible heaven) in Genesis 1 and the garden of Eden in Genesis 2 (outside

---

25. Philip Peter Jensen, *Graded Holiness: A Key to the Priestly Conception of the World* (Sheffield: JSOT Press, 1992), 89–114.

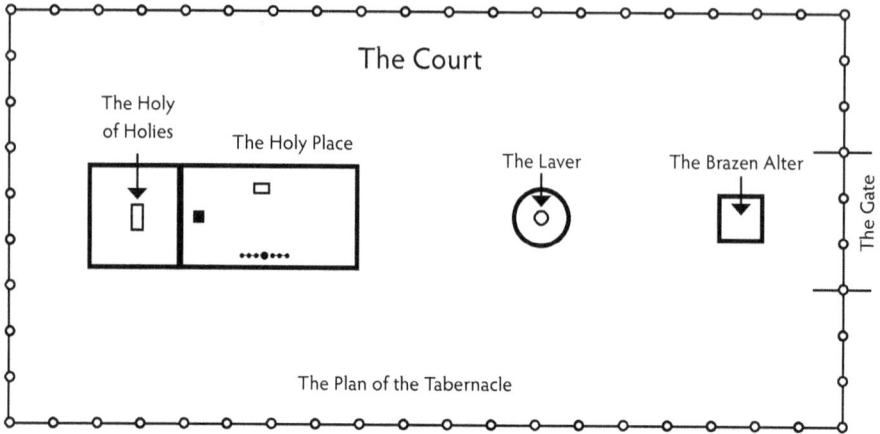

Figure 2.2

garden/garden/Eden).[26] After the creation of the world, God "rested" and dwelt with Adam and Eve in the middle of the garden.

The books of Exodus and Leviticus make it explicit that the tabernacle – and later, in 1 Kings, the Solomonic temple – was a microcosm of God's dwelling presence in the world. It was the physical sacred space because it was where God dwelled, represented by the coming of the glory of God in Exodus 40/1 Kings 8. It was God's inhabitation that made the space "sacred." Moreover, Exodus and Leviticus teach that while the cosmic world is sacred, the sacredness was manifested in at least two levels: the holy and the most holy, with the latter being where the ark of the covenant, the centre of holiness, was located. The degrees of sacredness are observable in the relationship between the cosmic world and the tabernacle.

Third Insight: The Metanarrative of a Journey in Proverbs

Another key insight from Proverbs is the metanarrative of the journey of the son as reflected in Proverbs 1–9. My thesis is that in this journey, the son is constantly warned by his wise parents to choose and pursue wisdom each step

---

26. G. K. Beale, *The Temple and the Church's Mission: A Biblical Theology of the Dwelling Place of God* (Downers Grove, IL: InterVarsity Press, 2004), 48, 75.

of the way until he reaches the final destination of dining with Lady Wisdom, who represents the sacred divine presence (Prov 9).

Let me demonstrate how this works.

Major Literary Divisions in Proverbs

The book of Proverbs is composed of thirty-one chapters. It has been divided into at least two major sections. Proverbs 1–9 is often demarcated from Proverbs 10–31 due to its different literary genre and style. The latter part is composed of single atomistic sentence-wisdom. The first part, Proverbs 1–9, is composed of bigger literary units or longer sections. They are referred to as "Instructions" or "Wisdom Poems." Most of these sections are prefaced with the reference to "my son," which is curiously absent in the second part. Proverbs scholars have considered the first section to be isolated poems and instructions unrelated to each other. However, I argue (see below) that the sections are compositionally related as they depict the journey of the son.

Moreover, the relationship between the two sections is that the first section provides the narrative framework, while the second section provides the wisdom aphorisms applicable in that narrative framework. The narrative framework is the necessary undergirding story or context that gives meaning and significance to the independent atomistic aphorisms.

The Imagery of a "Journey" in Proverbs 1–9

Observe the multiple elements constituting the narrative of journey in Proverbs 1–9. There is a collocation of *derek* "street," "path," and "way" language, which may mean (1) a physical road, (2) a journey or (3) a course of action. The wisdom is depicted like an amulet, providing protection from evil, tied on one's body or neck for the journey (1:8–9; 6:20–22; 3:21–23).

The collection describes the various people, activities and situations one encountered when on a journey during ancient times: road robbery and bandits in Proverbs 1:10–19; a tavern prostitute offering hospitality and inviting travellers to stay in her house in chapter 7; problems with fraudulent business transactions in 6:1–5. The collection describes the motivations/purpose for the journey: the pursuit of gold and silver through trade and commerce (3:14); the pursuit of healing (3:8); the pursuit of honour (3:16). Ancient road naming is also seen: roads are named according to their final destination – for example, "the way to life" and "the way of death"; or they are named according to their functions and travellers – for example, the "way of the wicked" and the "way of wisdom."

Finally, two ultimate destinations are in view. The structure and placement of Proverbs 9 is suggestive. I briefly discussed this earlier. Narratively, the chapter describes two destinations/fates of the son: either he ends up dining with Lady Wisdom (9:1–6) or he ends up with Lady Folly (9:13–18). As the son travels and chooses wisdom over folly, he reaches his final destination of dining with Wisdom, who is symbolic of the divine in Proverbs 9:1–6. However, if he chooses folly, he will enter the house of Lady Folly in Proverbs 9:13–18. The cultic life of Israel parallels this since they lived in the camps and later towns outside the tabernacle/temple which were considered to be the profane/common realm. An annual pilgrimage was designed for the Israelites to access the divine presence at the tabernacle/temple to worship and offer their sacrifices.

Movement and Progression from Sacred to More Sacred

Schwáb's discussion on "sanctifying the secular through wisdom" perceives choosing wisdom as static, fixed and stationary, in participating in the divine. I would like to develop his thesis further and argue that choosing wisdom should be placed in the context of a life journey that is reflected in Proverbs: a journey that involves a progressive movement which is forward-looking and wisdom-driven. Hence, wisdom may be understood as an increasing and progressing which is attained over time and is a movement from the sacred to the more sacred.

These progressive and increasing stages of wisdom are organic in the book, as seen in the following passages:

> Give instruction to the wise, and they will become wiser still;
>   teach the righteous and they will gain in learning.
> (Prov 9:9 NRSV)

Let the wise also hear and gain in learning,
> and the discerning acquire skill,
to understand a proverb and a figure,
> the words of the wise and their riddles [the already wise are ex-
> horted to continue hearing and to gain more learning, etc.].
(Prov 1:5–6 NRSV)

A scoffer seeks wisdom in vain,
> but knowledge is easy for one who understands [the discerning
> receive more knowledge].
(Prov 14:6 NRSV)

Thus, choosing wisdom as one's life journey is a progressive movement to reach a mature, deeper and comprehensive experiential knowledge of oneself, the world and the divine. It is a forward movement and not a static point. Wisdom is outside oneself and must be pursued tenaciously every day in one's life.

Analogically, the journey imagery invites the traveller to move forward *from* secular (if this label is to be maintained) *to/from* sacred *to* most sacred. By choosing wisdom rather than folly, the travelling son is invited and encouraged to enter the most sacred realm – the intimate dining experience with the divine.

Questions for Personal Reflection and Group Discussion

1. Reflect upon and discuss the author's proposal that, according to the categories and worldview of Proverbs, it is more accurate to speak of "the sacred and the more sacred" than the more commonly used "secular and sacred" dichotomy.

2. With relation to ourselves and those we teach in the church and seminary, what are some of the challenges involved in changing ingrained mental categories, presuppositions and worldviews? Apply this concept to particular individuals (perhaps without mentioning names in discussion).

3. What challenges might be involved in your particular context in beginning to interpret the world in terms of "sacred and more sacred" rather than "secular

and sacred," and in helping others to do the same? How might your culture differ from others as you go about this task?

4. What biblical and theological principles outside of Proverbs can be presented to support the "sacred and more sacred" view? For example, how would you relate these ideas to the Pauline concept of "flesh/spirit"?

5. If we contemplate all of the world as in some degree sacred (by virtue of being God's creation, inhabited by his omnipresence and imbued with common and saving grace, etc.), what implications does the "sacred and more sacred" worldview have for the way Christians understand and interact with elements commonly seen as secular (culture, arts, society, work, politics, etc.)?

6. Pause and give thanks for your favourite music, works of art, social activity, work activity.

7. What implications does the "sacred and more sacred" worldview have for redemptive mission that seeks to reclaim divine purposes in so-called "secular" aspects of life, in which God-given sanctity has been diminished through the effects of sin?

8. In what ways does the "sacred and more sacred" worldview confront and inform secular-sacred distinctions, common to evangelical churches and theological institutions, regarding ordained and lay ministry, and the diverse callings of Christians within the marketplace and society?

9. Pause to give thanks for new insights from this study. Pray for wisdom to implement personal and institutional changes from these insights.

References

Adams, Samuel L. *Wisdom in Transition: Act and Consequence in Second Temple Instructions.* Supplements to the Journal for the Study of Judaism 125. Leiden: Brill, 2008.

Beale, G. K. *The Temple and the Church's Mission: A Biblical Theology of the Dwelling Place of God.* Downers Grove, IL: InterVarsity Press, 2004.

Burchardt, Marian, Monika Wohlrab-Sahr and Matthias Middell, eds. *Multiple Secularities Beyond the West: Religion and Modernity in the Global Age*. Boston; Berlin; Munich: Walter de Gruyter, 2015.

Camp, Claudia V. *Wisdom and the Feminine in the Book of Proverbs*. Bible and Literature Series 11. Decatur, GA: Almond; Sheffield: JSOT Press, 1985.

Clifford, Richard, ed. *Wisdom Literature in Mesopotamia and Israel*. Society of Biblical Literature Symposium Series 36. Atlanta: SBL, 2007.

Dell, Katharine J. *The Book of Proverbs in Social and Theological Context*. Cambridge: Cambridge University Press, 2006.

Estes, Daniel J. *Hear, My Son: Teaching and Learning in Proverbs 1–9*. New Studies in Biblical Theology. Grand Rapids, MI: Eerdmans, 1997.

Fichtner, Johannes. *Die Altorientalische Weisheit in ihrer israelitisch-jüdischen Ausprägung*. Beihefte zur Zeitschrift für die Alttestamentliche Wissenschaft 62. Giessen: Alfred Töpelmann, 1933.

Forti, Tova L. "The *Isha Zara* in Proverbs 1–9: Allegory and Allegorization." *Hebrew Studies* 48 (2007): 89–100.

Fox, Michael. *Proverbs 1–9: A New Translation with Introduction and Commentary*. Anchor Bible 18A. New Haven: Yale University Press, 2009.

Jensen, Philip Peter. *Graded Holiness: A Key to the Priestly Conception of the World*. Sheffield: JSOT Press, 1992.

Kidner, Derek. *Proverbs: An Introduction and Commentary*. Tyndale Old Testament Commentaries. London: Tyndale, 1975.

Lambert, Wilfred G. *Babylonian Wisdom Literature*. Oxford: Clarendon, 1960.

McKane, William. *Proverbs: A New Approach*. Old Testament Library. Philadelphia: Westminster, 1970.

Rankin, O. S. *Israel's Wisdom Literature: Its Bearing on Theology and the History of Religion*. Edinburgh: T&T Clark, 1964.

Schwáb, Zoltán S. *Toward an Interpretation of the Book of Proverbs: Selfishness and Secularity Reconsidered*. Journal of Theological Interpretation Supplements 7. Winona Lake, IN: Eisenbrauns, 2013.

Taylor, Charles. *A Secular Age*. Cambridge, MA: Harvard University Press, 2007.

van Leeuwen, Raymond C. "Cosmos, Temple, House: Building and Wisdom in Mesopotamia and Israel." In *Wisdom Literature in Mesopotamia and Israel*, edited by Richard J. Clifford, 67–90. Atlanta: SBL, 2007.

Weeks, Stuart. *Instruction and Imagery in Proverbs 1–9*. Oxford: Oxford University Press, 2007.

Wells, David. *God in the Whirlwind: How the Holy-Love of God Reorients Our World.* Wheaton, IL: Crossway, 2014.

Westermann, Claus. *Roots of Wisdom: The Oldest Proverbs of Israel and Other Peoples.* Louisville, KY: Westminster John Knox, 1995.

Whybray, Roger Norman. *Wisdom in Proverbs.* Naperville: Alec Allenson, 1965.

Wilson, Frederick M. "Sacred and Profane? The Yahwistic Redaction of Proverbs Reconsidered." In *The Listening Heart: Essays in Wisdom and the Psalms in Honour of Roland E. Murphy, O. Carm,* edited by Kenneth G. Hugland, Elizabeth F. Huwiler, Jonathan T. Glass and Roger W. Lee, 313–334. Journal for the Study of the Old Testament Supplement Series 58. Sheffield: Sheffield Academic Press, 1987.

Wolters, Al. *The Song of the Valiant Woman: Studies in the Interpretation of Proverbs 31:1–21.* Carlisle: Paternoster, 2001.

Wright, G. E. *God Who Acts: Biblical Theology as Recital.* London: SCM, 1952.

Yoder, Christine Roy. *Wisdom as a Woman of Substance.* Beihefte zur Zeitschrift für die Alttestamentliche Wissenschaft 304. Berlin: de Gruyter, 2001.

Section 2

A Call for Virtue

In this section we feature three authors who make an appeal to the seminary for an integrated theological education. They appeal for attention less on the skills of ministry and more on the formation of persons to ready them for pastoral ministry – though even to express it in that way suggests a dichotomy which all argue against. They are seeking an integration of the person and the person-in-context, and thus an integration of the focal activities of theological education.

It has often been observed that the "selection criteria" for leadership in the Pastoral Epistles include just one skill, the capacity for teaching, and thereafter only state the requirements for the leader's character and behavioural traits. In these chapters that simplicity is supplemented with historical and educational theory that helps us interpret what it will take to achieve the biblical vision of qualified leaders.

The sacred-secular divide is exposed as part of a bigger negative tendency which can infect theological education. The Greek partitive approach to body and spirit is as influential as it is unhelpful in the formation of leaders for the church. A more holistic approach is needed, and our authors guide us towards such a vision.

Lily Chua's chapter follows on directly from the work by Ho on interpreting Proverbs. She uses the category results from Ho's work to emphasize that theological education is a movement from sacred to more sacred. She interrogates the very practical challenges of moral formation, such as the use of pornography by pastors, divorce rates, moral lapses, narcissism and church conflict. To help answer these she adapts Keller's cultural analysis (which sheds light on the sacred-secular divide) in line with Ho's Proverbs research and suggests a range of practical ways in which seminaries can appropriate these biblical insights.

Marvin Oxenham in chapter 4 proposes that just as theological education has in part led to the sacred-secular divide, so too it can be part of overcoming it. He challenges the church and its leaders to the transformation of culture through engagement with, and promotion of, character and virtue education. This will engage society, not just as a work of common grace, but also as part of the vehicle for fulfilling the *missio Dei*.

Marilyn Naidoo focuses on the idea of identity formation which helps answer the core questions of "Who am I?" and "What am I supposed to do?" She offers the model of Personality and Social Structure Perspective from House which has both a collective (socialization) and an individual (psychological) development concept. These are applied to theological education in order to strengthen the process of formation for pastoral leaders.

This section does not provide a complete response to the question "What might the seminary do to help overcome the sacred-secular divide?" It does, however, challenge seminaries to consider the totality of their educational offerings and processes, and as such is a clear call to holism.

3

Insights from Proverbs Applied in Theological Education

Lily K. Chua

This chapter builds on chapter 2 and continues the discussion on how the insights drawn from Proverbs can be applied in theological education. The core thesis is that formation in theological education is a progression to maturity in Christ among students and faculty from sacred to more sacred.

Theological Education in the Context of Formation: A Move from Sacred to More Sacred

In chapter 2, Ho has argued that "secular/sacred may be a categorical mistake, at least in Proverbs." She highlighted three thematic insights from Proverbs:

- First insight: Secular as neutral space – the international nature of Proverbs: *Wisdom as sanctifying the secular (Neutral)*
- Second insight: Secular as human autonomy/disenchantment: from secular/sacred divide to sacred/more sacred divide: *Wisdom as human agency (from secular/sacred divide to sacred/more sacred)*
- Third insight: The metanarrative of a journey progressing from periphery to the centre of divine presence: *Wisdom as movement and lifelong (progression to maturity from sacred to more sacred)*

I take this as a timely wake-up call. Formation from "sacred to more sacred" and "the lifelong journey of progression towards maturity" speak to the very heart of theological education. It is, in New Testament language, a maturing to conformity to Christ, and this is the mission of Christian education and of theological education.

Bridging the sacred-secular divide in some areas of our church life has inadvertently tilted in the direction of the secular. We proactively engage the secular to close the gap in the sacred-secular divide, but could it also be possible that we compromise the sacred in our active effort to bridge the two?

As presented below, results from church-related research make us wary of how we have been forming our seminary students. Moral lapses and narcissistic personalities among church pastors are on the rise, so we are pressured to assess our educational effectiveness: Have we been forming our students? Did it work? Do the ministerial and life outcomes of our seminary graduates reflect the mission of our schools and the purposes of theological education? In their life journeys, did they choose wisdom, or did they choose folly?

We may have a more pressing problem to face than addressing the sacred-secular divide problem.

Need for Formation in Moral Character: Moral Lapses

LifeWay Research[1] launched a qualitative study to identify factors that contribute to pastoral attrition. Factors identified included burnout, moral lapse, conflict in the church, a poor fit with the church, and family issues. In addition, three overarching themes emerge in the research: (1) demands and expectations; (2) need for fulfilment; and (3) spiritual and emotional health.

The research concludes that at the core of the interrelated attrition factors there is an underlying issue of spiritual health or insecurity, which when left unchecked manifests itself in forms such as burnout or a moral lapse.

This principle can be seen in recent research statistics on moral lapses related to pastors.

---

1. LifeWay Research, "Pastors More Likely to Address Domestic Violence, Still Lack Training," 18 September 2018, https://lifewayresearch.com/2018/09/18/pastors-more-likely-to-address-domestic-violence-still-lack-training/.

Pornography Statistics

First, in regard to pornography usage, reports from Barna[2] and Gallup[3] show a rapid change in moral perceptions among non-Christians and Christians alike. An increasing number of people are adopting a more permissive viewpoint on sexuality, sex and pornography. Barna notes that 14 percent of pastors and 21 percent of youth pastors claim they struggle with pornography. This means, one in five youth pastors and one in seven senior pastors utilize pornography on a regular basis and are currently struggling with shame and guilt.

This makes one wonder what percentage we would find if we studied the usage of pornography among seminarian students. To what degree is the use of pornography related to poorer spiritual health?

Divorce Rates

In the context of marriage, although several sources have disproved the conventional wisdom that divorce among believers is just as prevalent as among non-believers,[4] Christian marriage is still at stake.

Wright[5] wrote that cohabitation rates among evangelicals have quadrupled and divorce/separation rates have doubled since the 1970s. Krejcir,[6] in his ongoing research, found that 3 percent of Reformed and evangelical pastors self-reported having had an affair. Thus Stanton,[7] looking at the new statistics,

---

2. Barna Group and Josh McDowell Ministry, *The Porn Phenomenon* (Ventura: Barna, 2016), 80. See also Covenant Eyes, "The Porn Stat 2018," www.covenanteyes.com.

3. Gallup, "More Americans Say Pornography Is Morally Acceptable," 5 June 2018, https://news.gallup.com/poll/235280/americans-say-pornography-morally-acceptable.aspx.

4. Ed Stetzer, "Pastors: That Divorce Rate Stat You Quoted Was Probably Wrong," *Christianity Today*, 27 September 2012, https://www.christianitytoday.com/edstetzer/2012/september/pastors-that-divorce-rate-stat-you-quoted-was-probably.html; "Marriage, Divorce, and the Church: What Do the Stats Say, and Can Marriage Be Happy?," *Christianity Today*, 14 February 2014, https://www.christianitytoday.com/edstetzer/2014/february/marriage-divorce-and-body-of-christ-what-do-stats-say-and-c.html.

5. Bradley R. E. Wright, *Christians Are Hate-Filled Hypocrites . . . And Other Lies You've Been Told: A Sociologist Shatters Myths from the Secular and Christian Media* (Grand Rapids, MI: Baker, 2010).

6. Richard J. Krejcir, "Statistics on Pastors: 2016 Update," ChurchLeadership.org, 2016, http://www.churchleadership.org/apps/articles/default.asp?blogid=0&view=post&articleid=Statistics-on-Pastors-2016-Update&link=1&fldKeywords=&fldAuthor=&fldTopic=0.

7. Glenn Stanton, "Fact-Checker: Divorce Rate among Christians," Gospel Coalition, 25 September 2012, https://www.thegospelcoalition.org/article/factchecker-divorce-rate-among-christians.

concluded that "[the rate] is still higher than most of us are comfortable with." Indeed, we still have much room for improvement.

Sexual Misconduct

On top of the pornography statistics and divorce rates, the #MeToo movement, together with the #ChurchToo movement it prompted, has brought about unprecedented wake-up calls, discussion and confusion regarding the domestic violence, sexual abuse and sexual misconduct in evangelical circles. With the stepping down of prominent evangelical leaders since November 2017, the movements have demonstrated the magnitude of the inherent institutional problems in parachurch organizations, churches and seminaries.

The statement "silence is not spiritual" has awakened the evangelical community to undertake and confront the institutionalized effort to silence victims abused by people of authority such as pastors, ministers and seminary leaders.

Reflection

In my home, Taiwan, we have a dearth of research on sexual harassment in the church. There are no reliable statistics available on pastoral sexual misconduct. Yet from different denominations, in different parts of the island and in different sections of Taiwan churches, we have heard of pastors or Christian leaders who had inappropriate liaisons with people under their trust and/or were accused of committing a variety of sexual offences.

Churches and seminaries need resources and training to address the issue of moral lapses. What measures can we take at the early stage of theological training to prevent harm from happening? What processes need to be in place for students to aspire to a higher level of sacredness as well as to pursue holiness over their lifetime? The absence of a separation from these secular choices, evidenced in recent allegations of pastoral sexual misconduct, is for us a call to action, albeit under unwelcome circumstances.

To further the problem, research points us not only to the need for formation in moral character among pastors-to-be, but also to the need for formation in Christian virtues among ministers and seminarians.

Need for Formation in Christian Virtues: Narcissistic Tendencies

Raskin and Terry[8] identified various components of narcissism in the inventory they developed for Narcissistic Personality Disorder (NPD). These include authority, self-sufficiency, superiority, exhibitionism, exploitativeness, vanity and entitlement. After using the NPD inventory with celebrities, Pinsky and Young[9] argued that most particularly it is the scores reflected for vanity, entitlement, exhibitionism and exploitativeness that are the greatest cause for concern.

Researchers have consistently confirmed that components of narcissism in leaders bring damage to the institutions they lead. Narcissistic pastors show a need for power, control, praise and public recognition. They often have hidden anger problems and therefore are difficult to work with and relate to within a relationship.

Narcissism[10] and Church Conflicts

Puls, Ball and Sandage[11] studied a large Canadian denomination and found a connection between clergy narcissism and destructive church conflicts. To their surprise, they found a relatively higher percentage of clergy meeting the diagnostic criteria of Narcissistic Personality Disorder (NPD) than in the regular population.

Puls and Ball warn that Narcissistic Personality Disorder, in its overt or covert forms, often hides behind layers of "sacred" deception. The researchers

---

8. Robert Raskin and Howard Terry, "A Principal-Components Analysis of the Narcissistic Personality Inventory and Further Evidence of Its Construct Validity," *Journal of Personality and Social Psychology* 54, no. 5 (1988): 890–902.

9. Drew Pinsky and S. Mark Young, *The Mirror Effect: How Celebrity Narcissism Is Seducing America* (Audiobook; New York: HarperAudio, 2009).

10. The focus here is on the social-personality trait of narcissism and not on the diagnostic trait.

11. R. Glenn Ball and Darrell Puls, "Frequency of Narcissistic Personality Disorder in Pastors: A Preliminary Study," paper presented to the American Association of Christian Counselors, Nashville, 26 September 2015, http://www.darrellpuls.com/images/AACC_2015_Paper_NPD_in_Pastors.pdf; R. Glenn Ball, Darrell Puls and Steven J. Sandage, *Let Us Pray: The Plague of Narcissist Pastors and What We Can Do about It* (Eugene, OR: Wipf & Stock, 2017).

also found that, when compared with the non-NPDs, the NPD pastors engage in markedly fewer spiritual disciplines and interactive ministry practices.

Narcissism and Other Constructs

Sandage and Harden[12] reported that narcissism negatively correlates with intercultural competence. Such competence involves "the ability to think and act in interculturally appropriate ways"[13] and is vital for helping professionals to relate and care without prejudice.

Similarly, Cooper, Pullig and Dickens[14] found that narcissism impacts the ethical judgment required for effective church leadership. As leaders of the church, ministers frequently deal with ethical issues that need decision-making. However, an inflated sense of self-importance, an obsessive desire for admiration and a lack of empathy with others impair ethical judgment and result in questionable decisions.

Lastly, Pan[15] argued that individualistic culture is the source of increasing narcissistic leanings among seminarians and ministers. Similarly, as Pinsky and Young[16] in their study of narcissism among celebrities observed, celebrity culture is making the average young person more narcissistic.

Reflection

My seminary, China Evangelical Seminary, marked its sixtieth anniversary in 2020. Many of our alumni in the early days stayed in the same ministry for twenty to thirty years and churches grew in their care. By contrast, in the last five years we have seen more frequent pastorate-changing, and even increasing numbers of pastors leaving the ministry, among our more recent students.

12. Steven J. Sandage and Mark G. Harden, "Relational Spirituality, Differentiation of Self, and Virtue as Predictors of Intercultural Development," *Mental Health, Religion & Culture* 14, no. 8 (2011): 819–838.

13. Sandage and Harden, "Relational Spirituality," 819.

14. Marjorie J. Cooper, Chris J. Pullig and Charles W. Dickens, "Effects of Narcissism and Religiosity on Church Ministers with Respect to Ethical Judgment, Confidence, and Forgiveness," *Journal of Psychology & Theology* 44, no. 1 (2016): 42–54.

15. Shinhwan Pan, "Pastoral Counselling of Korean Clergy with Burnout: Culture and Narcissism," *The Asia Journal of Theology* 20, no. 2 (2006): 241–255.

16. Pinsky and Young, *Mirror Effect.*

If pastoral attrition is related to church conflict, burnout and/or moral lapse, and these in turn are related to poor spiritual health and related narcissistic leanings, then what can be done and how can we help before damage is done to these pastors and the churches they serve?

We have yet to study the factors that contribute to such phenomena. But perhaps it is justifiable to inquire to what degree we as leaders and trainers of the students have contributed to the separation they displayed between their knowledge and their lives. Have we inculcated a movement from the sacred to the more sacred? Have we lived out the true division between life by the flesh and life by the Spirit?

Need for Formation: Common Awareness among Theological Schools

In 2018 the Association of Theological Schools (ATS) published part of the findings from their $7 million Lilly-funded Educational Models and Practices Project.[17] Part of the project aimed to explore and assess particular educational models and practices within their 270-member schools. For this purpose, eighteen peer groups, including more than 200 representatives from 110 schools, convened from 2015 to 2017.

One of the key findings was that among the many issues raised, two-thirds of the eighteen peer groups addressed the issue of formation in their discussions and reports. While the definition of formation was quite diverse, in most instances the reference of formation was to personal and spiritual formation.

ATS Senior Director Stephen R. Graham (2018) wrote, "Many are recognizing a shift from a focus on professional theological education (education for the profession of ministry), to the *formation of persons* to serve in an array of roles of religious leadership" (emphasis added).[18]

---

17. The Association of Theological Schools, *Explore, Assess, Affirm: The ATS Educational Models and Practices Project; Educational Models and Practices Peer Group Final Reports* (2018), https://www.ats.edu/uploads/resources/current-initiatives/educational-models/publications-and-presentations/peer-group-final-reports/peer-group-final-report-book.pdf.

18. Stephen R. Graham, "Educational Models and Practices: What We've Learned and Why It Matters," The Association of Theological Schools (ATS) Biennial Meeting, Denver, CO, 20 June 2018, https://www.ats.edu/uploads/resources/current-initiatives/educational-models/publications-and-presentations/ed-models-biennial-pres-text-2018.pdf.

ATS accreditor Tom Tanner also offered his thoughts when he noted that ATS in the past has tended to treat theological education primarily as a profession. He wrote, "As ATS enters its second century, the next set of standards may need to focus more on formation as an overarching goal of theological education."[19]

Evidently, theological schools have come to realize that other than intellectual/academic and ministerial/pastoral formation, there should be a balanced emphasis on personal and spiritual formation.

Models of Sacred-Secular Divide in Theological Education

In chapter 2, Ho started with the definitions of what is sacred and secular. This is crucial, as we have different definitions and understandings when addressing the issue of the sacred-secular divide. Such differences are not surprising because at the root of our differences is the very question of how we engage culture.

As early as 1956, Niebuhr laid out five models for how Christians have related Christ to culture throughout history. More recently, Keller[20] renamed and refined Niebuhr's models into four basic ways of how churches relate to culture.

While models are never perfect categorizations of differences, Keller reasoned that usage of models would help us avoid extremes and imbalances. Each of these models, Keller argued, has grasped "a motif or guiding biblical truth that helps Christians relate to culture."[21] Consequently, when each is taken independently, it lacks something the other models capture and emphasize.

In this section, I will introduce Keller's four views and how they can be applied to our sacred-secular divide conversations.

---

19. Tom Tanner, "Reflections on Key Themes and Principles from ATS Peer Groups," The Association of Theological Schools, 16 August 2018, https://www.ats.edu/uploads/resources/current-initiatives/economic-challenges-facing-future-ministers/peer-group-reports-themes-and-principles.pdf.
20. Timothy Keller, *Center Church: Doing Balanced, Gospel-Centered Ministry in Your City* (Grand Rapids, MI: Zondervan, 2012).
21. Keller, *Center Church*, 195.

Keller's Four Views

Keller described four ways of relating to culture. They are "the Transformationists," "the Relevants," "the Two Kingdoms" and "the Counterculturalists."
Succinctly understood,

- The *Transformationists* aim to penetrate and transform culture by
  calling the church to live out the Christian worldview in every sphere
  of life.
- The *Relevants,* however, believe that God is already at work in
  culture and therefore Christ's church is not to transform but to
  be more sensitive and relevant by joining and learning from the
  surrounding culture.
- The *Counterculturalists,* on the other hand, believe that the best thing
  the church can do for the world is to exhibit Christ's kingdom as
  an alternative human society to the world. There is no hope for the
  culture to be transformed.
- And lastly, the *Two Kingdoms* model sees the church as citizens of the
  earthly kingdom as well as of the redemptive kingdom. Since both
  are ruled by God, Christians should fulfil different responsibilities
  in each, and in an excellent way.

Keller's Two Questions

For Keller, the fundamental differences between these four ways of cultural
engagement can be reduced to two questions:

- First, should we be pessimistic or optimistic about the possibility
  of cultural change?
- And second, is the current culture redeemable and good, or
  fundamentally fallen?

Briefly, if one is optimistic about cultural change but sees culture as fallen,
then one will probably adopt the Transformationist model. On the other hand,
if one is optimistic about cultural change and sees culture as good, then one
will probably adopt the Relevant model.

If one is pessimistic about cultural change but sees culture as good, then
one will probably adopt the Two Kingdoms model. Finally, if one is pessimistic

about cultural change and sees culture as fallen, then one will probably adopt the Counterculturalist model.

Application of Keller's Four Views

In my attempt to apply Keller's frameworks to our discussion on the sacred-secular divide in theological education, the models may look as shown in figure 3.1.

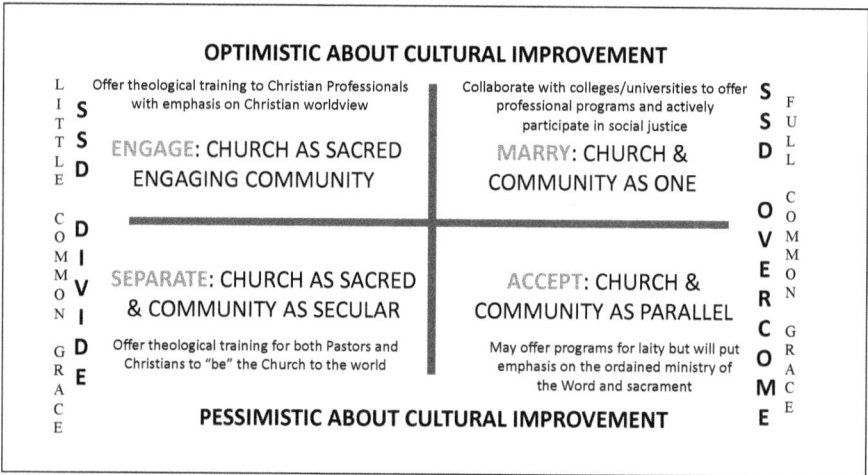

OPTIMISTIC ABOUT CULTURAL IMPROVEMENT

Offer theological training to Christian Professionals with emphasis on Christian worldview

ENGAGE: CHURCH AS SACRED ENGAGING COMMUNITY

Collaborate with colleges/universities to offer professional programs and actively participate in social justice

MARRY: CHURCH & COMMUNITY AS ONE

SEPARATE: CHURCH AS SACRED & COMMUNITY AS SECULAR

Offer theological training for both Pastors and Christians to "be" the Church to the world

ACCEPT: CHURCH & COMMUNITY AS PARALLEL

May offer programs for laity but will put emphasis on the ordained ministry of the Word and sacrament

PESSIMISTIC ABOUT CULTURAL IMPROVEMENT

(Left axis labels: LITTLE COMMON GRACE; SSD; DIVIDE)

(Right axis labels: SSD; OVERCOME; FULL COMMON GRACE)

Figure 3.1 Application of Keller's Four Views to Conversations on SSD

If the institutional leaders are optimistic about cultural change but see culture as secular and something to be redeemed, then they will probably adopt the "Divide but Engage" model and will offer theological training to Christian professionals with an emphasis on the Christian worldview for them to transform the world at work. This they do without sacrificing their primary mission to train students preparing for full-time ministry.

If the institutional leaders are optimistic about cultural change and see culture as sacred where God is at work, then they will probably adopt the "Overcome and Marry" model. They will advocate for collaboration with colleges and universities to offer professional programs in addition to their theological programs. Also, their faculty and students will actively participate in social justice for the common good of all.

If the institutional leaders are pessimistic about cultural change but see culture as sacred due to God's common grace, then they will probably adopt the "Overcome and Accept" model. They may decide to offer programs for laity to excel in their secular vocations, but will put emphasis on the ordained ministry of the Word and sacrament.

Lastly, if the institutional leaders are pessimistic about cultural change and see culture as secular, then they will probably adopt the "Divide and Separate" model and will offer theological training for both pastors and Christians so they may be formed and be the church to the world.

Reflection

If, as Keller argued, each of the above models contains an *essential truth about church and culture*, yet at the same time overlooks some implications of the creation, the fall, the redemption and the restoration themes in the biblical storyline, then it is paramount for us to ask: What is the way ahead?

How do we proceed? Which model should we choose? Do we adopt all models in doing theological education? If so, do we have the needed resources to do everything? Or do we do things differently at different stages or seasons in the cycle of the church's relationship to culture? What is the primary mission for us as theological institutions?

In the final section, I will present an adaptation of Keller's framework and propose how insights drawn from Proverbs by Ho in chapter 2 can be integrated into our conversation about sacred and secular.

A Proposal: Formation from Sacred to More Sacred

Keller admonishes, "Seek the centre"; "blend the cultural and biblical insights of all the models" into actual practice and ministry.[22] Keller also suggests, "Follow your gifts and calling." In other words, choose which one does best with all the resources and opportunities given.

---

22. Keller, *Center Church*, 238. Briefly, when applied to our theological context, this means teaching a *distinctive worldview*, caring for the *common good* of all, valuing *humble excellence* and equipping the church to *counter culture*. Keller writes, "The biblical material calls for a balance not of compromises but of 'being controlled simultaneously and all the time' by all of the teaching in Scripture," 230.

Thus, drawing on insights from Proverbs, I here propose the structure shown in figure 3.2.

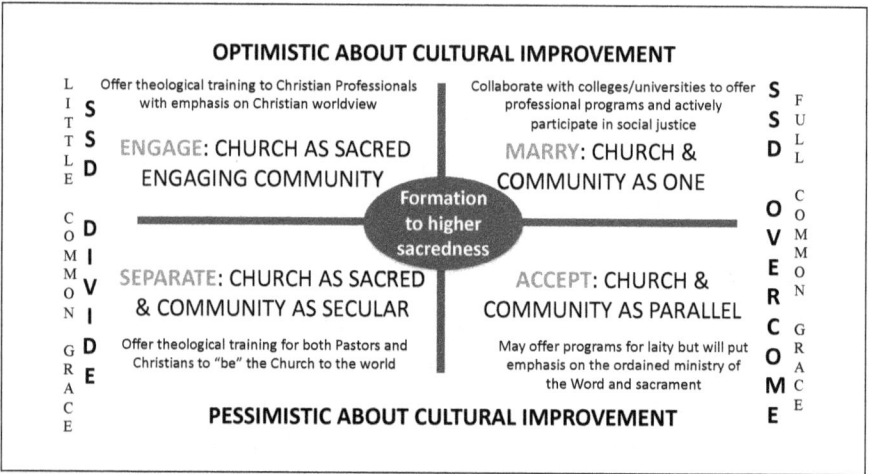

OPTIMISTIC ABOUT CULTURAL IMPROVEMENT

Offer theological training to Christian Professionals with emphasis on Christian worldview	Collaborate with colleges/universities to offer professional programs and actively participate in social justice
ENGAGE: CHURCH AS SACRED ENGAGING COMMUNITY	**MARRY: CHURCH & COMMUNITY AS ONE**
SEPARATE: CHURCH AS SACRED & COMMUNITY AS SECULAR	**ACCEPT: CHURCH & COMMUNITY AS PARALLEL**
Offer theological training for both Pastors and Christians to "be" the Church to the world	May offer programs for laity but will put emphasis on the ordained ministry of the Word and sacrament

Formation to higher sacredness

PESSIMISTIC ABOUT CULTURAL IMPROVEMENT

Figure 3.2 Insights from Proverbs of SSD in Theological Education

Regardless of which model we use, think of ways in which students and faculty can be inspired, helped and formed to graduate from the sacred to the more sacred and to pursue a journey of lifelong progression towards maturity in Christ.

We hear Wisdom saying in Proverbs 9:5–6 (ESV):

Come, eat of my bread
and drink of the wine I have mixed.
Leave your simple ways, and live,
and walk in the way of insight.

And we hear repeated messages throughout the Scriptures:

. . . and you shall be to me a kingdom of priests and a holy nation. (Exod 19:6 ESV)

For I am the LORD who brought you up out of the land of Egypt to be your God. You shall therefore be holy, for I am holy. (Lev 11:45 ESV)

For you are a people holy to the LORD your God, and the LORD
has chosen you to be a people for his treasured possession, out of
all the peoples who are on the face of the earth.
(Deut 14:2 ESV)

Put on then, as God's chosen ones, holy and beloved, compassionate
hearts, kindness, humility, meekness, and patience.
(Col 3:12 ESV)

For this is the will of God, your sanctification: that you abstain
from sexual immorality . . . For God has not called us for impurity,
but in holiness.
(1 Thess 4:3–7 ESV)

But you are a chosen race, a royal priesthood, a holy nation, a people
for his own possession, that you may proclaim the excellencies of
him who called you out of darkness into his marvellous light.
(1 Pet 2:9 ESV)

So what does this formational framework look like in correspondence
with insights from Proverbs?

Formation Is Identifying That Which Is Neutral/Secular and Bringing It to Christ

This implies that our institutions need to move from *a program-oriented
emphasis to a purpose-oriented emphasis*. For example:

- *Divide and Separate* (counterculture): Bringing the laity, the "natural"
  person, to Christ.
- *Divide and Engage* (distinctive worldview): Bringing the mind and
  everyday living to Christ.
- *Overcome and Marry* (common good): Bringing all disciplines of
  study to Christ.
- *Overcome and Accept* (humble excellence): Bringing everyday
  profession to Christ.

Weekly Reality Check: Overcoming Pornography

In our seminary, as with most theological schools in Asia, we adopt the traditional residential mode of education. Faculty and students reside on campus, worshipping together as a community on a weekly basis and sharing meals provided on campus. Each faculty member is responsible for mentoring a student group of ten to twelve students who come together weekly for prayers, outings and meals.

Students are encouraged to share their "Weekly Reality Check" with their group mentor. This simple checklist of green, yellow and red dots shows items that are mundane and relate to everyday living, such as daily devotions, family/peer relationships, physical health, emotional health and sexual integrity.

We have had positive experiences with several students using this checklist. As they worked week after week on their checklists, they became aware of the interrelatedness of the items involved. The seemingly "natural" or "mundane" things are related to their spiritual health.

One of the students wrote: "Thank you for walking with me this past year. Indeed, I really need to get back to God." By God's grace, having gone through a whole year of accountability within a trusted advisor relationship, he has recovered from his pornography addiction without relapse.

Formation Is a Progression from Intellectual and Pastoral Emphases to a Balance across Four Dimensions: Intellectual, Pastoral, Personal and Spiritual

This implies progression from cognitive-based teaching to holistic-engagement learning; from task-fulfilment to self-motivated commitments; from self-centredness to God- and others-centredness; and from spiritual rituals/habits to self-disciplined devotion.

SPA Groups and DJ: Transitioning to Self-Disciplined Devotion

Years ago, our then Student Council started a project called "SPA" that has continued to this day. These Spiritual Partners Accountability (SPA) groups consist of three to four students who come together for weekly prayer, mutual support and accountability. They are student-initiated and student-monitored. This semester, in conjunction with the SPA groupings, the present Student

Council added another initiative called "DJ." They encourage the whole student body to write a Daily Journal as they observe their daily devotions.

As teachers and leaders of the student body, we are humbled to see such culture-making movements happening among our students. And we pray that the Holy Spirit, who alone can renew Christ's people to higher sacredness, will be pleased to utilize these peer-to-peer mentoring and supporting initiatives to help transform outward spiritual rituals into authentic inward devotion and love for Christ and his church.

Research is showing that unlike in the past, many students are entering graduate theological study without formation by networks of institutions. As a result, schools are "faced with the need for remedial work."[23] At our seminary, we continue to witness such need for remedial work. But in God's mercy, we also see his Spirit at work.

Formation is central to theological education. We need a more balanced formation of intellectual, ministerial, spiritual and character, forming students from task-fulfilment to self-motivated commitments, from self-centeredness to God- and others-centredness, and from spiritual rituals/habits to self-disciplined devotion.

Formation Is Lifelong Progression to Maturity in Christ from Life by the Flesh to Life by the Spirit

This implies progression from school-based learning to self-initiated lifelong learning; from individual devotion to faith-community building; and from church-community ministry to culture-making participation.

Student Character Formation: A Life-Long Progression

Christian virtues and character are compatible with true spiritual disciplines. In fact, they are formed out of spiritual disciplines, daily devotion, prayer groups, worship services and accountability relationships.

Formation is slow. It requires daily exercising of spiritual disciplines. It also demands, as Ho wrote in chapter 3, "a progressive movement which is forward-looking and wisdom-driven" towards the sacred, resulting in what Martin Luther called "a daily dying and rising with Christ."

---

23. Association of Theological Schools, *Explore, Assess, Affirm*.

Leading expert on forgiveness and Christian psychologist Worthington writes, "The essence of most virtues is that they self-limit the rights or privileges of the self on behalf of the welfare of others."[24] And well-respected Christian psychologist and researcher Mark McMinn[25] noted that all Christian virtues – forgiveness, gratitude, humility, hope, grace and wisdom – boil down to what the Lord commanded: "Love the Lord with all your heart . . . and love your neighbour." This implies that these virtues are truly possible only with people who have Christ's new life.

How then can we train and form our students to actualize these virtues?

Like other theological schools, Chinese Evangelical Seminary still has a long way to go. However, here are some processes we have been working hard on in the past few years to form our students:

1. Adhere to a rigorous entrance screening process that includes recommendation letters, written examination, a personality test and a face-to-face interview.

2. Administer the T-JTA Personality Test for all new students so they have enough time to work on their own temperament issues while at school. Test results are shared with each student on a one-on-one basis.

3. Require church participation in terms of weekend field education so students continue to take part in church ministries and have opportunities to sharpen their pastoring, teaching and caring skills.

4. Emphasize integration of knowledge and life/ministry through coursework, story-sharing and actual life examples.

5. Involve in-field supervisors in their students' lives and ministries through end-of-semester feedback and forms.

6. Design weekly meal-serving and campus-cleaning for students to practise servanthood.

7. Mandate utilization of outside-school professional counselling services so that students can deal with their unresolved life issues and by God's

---

24. Everett L. Worthington, Jr., "What Are the Different Dimensions of Humility?," Big Questions Online, 4 November 2014, https://answptest2.dreamhosters.com/2014/11/04/what-are-the-different-dimensions-of-humility/.

25. Mark McMinn, *The Science of Virtue: Why Positive Psychology Matters to the Church* (Grand Rapids, MI: Brazos, 2017).

grace experience healing and growth. Reflection papers are required for each of the four sessions in which they participate.

8. Administer NPD Personality Test during students' graduating year for students to self-check before exiting school.

9. Each semester, schedule teacher-student appointments and conduct monthly guidance group meetings for teachers to exchange observations and ideas regarding students needing extra help and care.

10. Understand the role of theological schools as only "one part of the full life span of Christian/theological education."[26]

In speaking about bringing people from the sacred to the more sacred, we are still very limited, but as Parker Palmer defines teaching, "to teach is to create a space in which obedience to truth is practiced."[27] We create space; God's Spirit does the work.

Questions for Personal Reflection and Group Discussion

1. Share your personal convictions regarding cultural engagement in response to the two questions posed by Keller:

- Should we be pessimistic or optimistic about the possibility for cultural change?
- Is the current culture redeemable and good, or fundamentally fallen?

Discuss the strengths and weaknesses of the four models for relating to culture that Keller describes: the Transformationists, the Relevants, the Two Kingdoms and the Counterculturalists. Which best reflects your own convictions? Are there aspects of another model that might serve as a complement to the model you have chosen?

2. At some times and in some places evangelicals have retreated from cultural engagement. At other times they have engaged deeply. Where has your faith tradition, theological institution and own ministry been positioned on this

---

26. Association of Theological Schools, *Explore, Assess, Affirm.*

27. Parker J. Palmer, *To Know as We Are Known: Education as a Spiritual Journey* (San Francisco: HarperOne, 1993), 69.

issue, and in practice? How have these positions impacted praxis regarding the nature of ministry, the scope of mission and the shape of theological education?

3. Do you sit comfortably within the majority of those around you? Or are you in a minority on these issues? What is that experience like for you and those around you?

4. Discuss and evaluate the author's thesis: "Formation in theological education is a progression to maturity in Christ among students and faculty *from sacred to more sacred*."

5. What does the phrase "from sacred to more sacred" add to your understanding of the type of development that Chua envisions for students and faculty, and the way that this formation relates to the so-called "secular" world?

6. Give thanks for the insights gained from this chapter and discussion. Pray for strength to change or to persevere. Pray for your society and for Christ's return.

References

The Association of Theological Schools. *Explore, Assess, Affirm: The ATS Educational Models and Practices Project; Educational Models and Practices Peer Group Final Reports.* 2018. https://www.ats.edu/uploads/resources/current-initiatives/educational-models/publications-and-presentations/peer-group-final-reports/peer-group-final-report-book.pdf.

Ball, R. Glenn, and Darrell Puls. "Frequency of Narcissistic Personality Disorder in Pastors: A Preliminary Study." Paper presented to the American Association of Christian Counselors, Nashville. 26 September 2015. http://www.darrellpuls.com/images/AACC_2015_Paper_NPD_in_Pastors.pdf.

Ball, R. Glenn, Darrell Puls and Steven J. Sandage. *Let Us Pray: The Plague of Narcissist Pastors and What We Can Do about It.* Eugene, OR: Wipf & Stock, 2017.

Barna Group, and Josh McDowell Ministry. *The Porn Phenomenon: The Impact of Pornography in the Digital Age.* Ventura: Barna, 2016.

Cooper, Marjorie J., Chris J. Pullig and Charles W. Dickens. "Effects of Narcissism and Religiosity on Church Ministers with Respect to Ethical Judgment, Confidence, and Forgiveness." *Journal of Psychology & Theology* 44, no. 1 (2016): 42–54.

Covenant Eyes. Porn Stat 2018. Pdf downloaded from https://www.covenanteyes.com/pornstats/?clickid=Ucu1ygx1SxyLULbwUx0Mo3wGUkExRoVQ7ys2Rw0&

irgwc=1&utm_source=IR&utm_medium=123201&utm_campaign=Online%20 Tracking%20Link&utm_size=&utm_type=ONLINE_TRACKING_LINK.

Dugan, Andrew. "More Americans Say Pornography Is Morally Acceptable." Gallup, 5 June 2018. https://news.gallup.com/poll/235280/americans-say-pornography-morally-acceptable.aspx.

Graham, Stephen R. "Educational Models and Practices: What We've Learned and Why It Matters." The Association of Theological Schools (ATS) Biennial Meeting, Denver, CO, 20 June 2018. https://www.ats.edu/uploads/resources/current-initiatives/educational-models/publications-and-presentations/ed-models-biennial-pres-text-2018.pdf.

Keller, Timothy. *Center Church: Doing Balanced, Gospel-Centered Ministry in Your City*. Grand Rapids, MI: Zondervan, 2012.

Krejcir, Richard J. "Statistics on Pastors: 2016 Update." ChurchLeadership.org. 2016. http://www.churchleadership.org/apps/articles/default.asp?blogid=0&view=post&articleid=Statistics-on-Pastors-2016-Update&link=1&fldKeywords=&fldAuthor=&fldTopic=0.

LifeWay Research. "Pastors More Likely to Address Domestic Violence, Still Lack Training. 18 September 2018. https://lifewayresearch.com/2018/09/18/pastors-more-likely-to-address-domestic-violence-still-lack-training/.

McMinn, Mark. *The Science of Virtue: Why Positive Psychology Matters to the Church*. Grand Rapids, MI: Brazos, 2017.

Palmer, Parker J. *To Know as We Are Known: Education as a Spiritual Journey*. San Francisco: HarperOne, 1993.

Pan, Shinhwan. "Pastoral Counselling of Korean Clergy with Burnout: Culture and Narcissism." *The Asia Journal of Theology* 20, no. 2 (2006): 241–255.

Pinsky, Drew, and S. Mark Young. *The Mirror Effect: How Celebrity Narcissism Is Seducing America*. Audiobook. New York: HarperAudio, 2009.

Raskin, Robin, and Howard Terry. "A Principal-Components Analysis of the Narcissistic Personality Inventory and Further Evidence of Its Construct Validity." *Journal of Personality and Social Psychology* 54, no. 5 (1988): 890–902.

Rector, John M. *Objectification Spectrum: Understanding and Transcending Our Diminishment and Dehumanization of Others*. New York: Oxford University Press, 2014.

Sandage, Steven J., and Mark G. Harden. "Relational Spirituality, Differentiation of Self, and Virtue as Predictors of Intercultural Development." *Mental Health, Religion & Culture* 14, no. 8 (2011): 819–838.

Smietana, Bob. "The #MeToo Movement Has Educated Pastors. And Left Them with More Questions." *Christianity Today*, 18 September 2018. https://www. christianitytoday.com/news/2018/september/metoo-domestic-violence-sexual-abuse-pastors-lifeway-2018.html.

Stanton, Glenn. "Fact-Checker: Divorce Rate among Christians." Gospel Coalition, 25 September 2012. https://www.thegospelcoalition.org/article/factchecker-divorce-rate-among-christians.

Stetzer, Ed. "Marriage, Divorce, and the Church: What Do the Stats Say, and Can Marriage Be Happy?" *Christianity Today*, 14 February 2014. https://www. christianitytoday.com/edstetzer/2014/february/marriage-divorce-and-body-of-christ-what-do-stats-say-and-c.html.

———. "Pastors: That Divorce Rate Stat You Quoted Was Probably Wrong." *Christianity Today*, 27 September 2012. https://www.christianitytoday.com/edstetzer/2012/september/pastors-that-divorce-rate-stat-you-quoted-was-probably.html.

Tanner, Tom. "Reflections on Key Themes and Principles from ATS Peer Groups." The Association of Theological Schools. 16 August 2018. https://www.ats.edu/uploads/resources/current-initiatives/economic-challenges-facing-future-ministers/peer-group-reports-themes-and-principles.pdf.

Worthington, Everett L., Jr. "What Are the Different Dimensions of Humility?" Big Questions Online. 4 November 2014. https://answptest2.dreamhosters.com/2014/11/04/what-are-the-different-dimensions-of-humility/.

Wright, Bradley R. E. *Christians Are Hate-Filled Hypocrites . . . And Other Lies You've Been Told: A Sociologist Shatters Myths from the Secular and Christian Media*. Grand Rapids, MI: Baker, 2010.

4

Bridging the Sacred-Secular Divide through Character and Virtue Education

Marvin Oxenham

In this chapter, we assume that there is a problematic sacred-secular divide in Christian theology and practice. We also recognize that theological education is partially responsible for generating and maintaining this divide and that, as such, it can be a unique part of the solution. In particular, we will explore how theological education can help bridge the sacred-secular divide through character and virtue education.

The perspective in our exploration will be both backward- and forward-looking. We will first look back at how the tradition of character and virtue education has been shared by secular philosophers and by Christian theologians and consider how this can represent a powerful meeting point. We will then consider how character and virtue education represents an objective that is shared today both by secular society and by the Christian *missio Dei*. In this shared objective we can find a new face of Christian apologetics and a solid bridge between the sacred and the secular.

Prolegomena
Prolegomenon 1: About Common Grace

Two issues need to be addressed by way of prolegomena. The first is about God and grace, and the second is about a selection of specialized words that are going to be used in the argument.

Concerning the first issue, the question is about how the grace of God operates in the secular world (the question might also be framed in terms of God's exercise of sovereignty outside the church). To be clear, the question is not about salvific grace but about common grace, seen as goodness that God gives the world as humanity continues a creational mandate and generates culture.[1] The point of reference in this discussion is surely Niebuhr's *Christ and Culture*, but Abraham Kuyper's vision of sphere sovereignty, presented in *Common Grace: God's Gifts for a Fallen World*, also represents an authoritative contribution. Richard Mouw[2] aptly summarizes three models that lead to Kuyper's vision of common grace, pictured in figure 4.1.

A first model presupposes that God's grace operates in the world exclusively *through the church*. Here, the church is considered as the sole mediator between God and the world, and thus anything that God wishes to do in culture, education, law or politics must pass through the church. This model is found in many faith traditions, and it is well exemplified by the Catholic enterprise in establishing Christian schools, Christian political parties, Christian publishers, and so on.

A second model suggests instead that God is at work only in the church. This model generates the harshest division between the sacred and the secular because it is founded on a vision of depravity and abandonment and claims that God's grace does not operate in culture nor can it be found in the secular

---

1. "The common grace of Kuyper was merely a favour of God that gives the world 'the temporal blessings' of rain, sunshine, health, and riches, and that restrains corruption in the world so that the world can produce good culture. It was not a grace that aimed at the salvation of the reprobate, a grace that was expressed in a well-meaning offer of Christ, or a grace that was grounded in a universal atonement" (Engelsma, in G. P. Johnson, "The Myth of Common Grace," *The Trinity Review*, March/April 1987, 6; accessed 27 November 2018, http://trinityfoundation.org/PDF/The%20Trinity%20Review%200055a%20TheMythofCommonGrace.pdf.

2. See Richard J. Mouw, "Some Reflections on Sphere Sovereignty," in *Religion, Pluralism and Public Life: Abraham Kuyper's Legacy for the Twenty-First Century*, ed. Luis E. Lugo (Grand Rapids, MI: Eerdmans, 2000), 160–182.

sciences. This model is ironically shared by secular society, which is quite happy to relegate God to the realm of religion and to claim total autonomy in all other spheres of knowledge and life.

ABOUT GOD AND GRACE

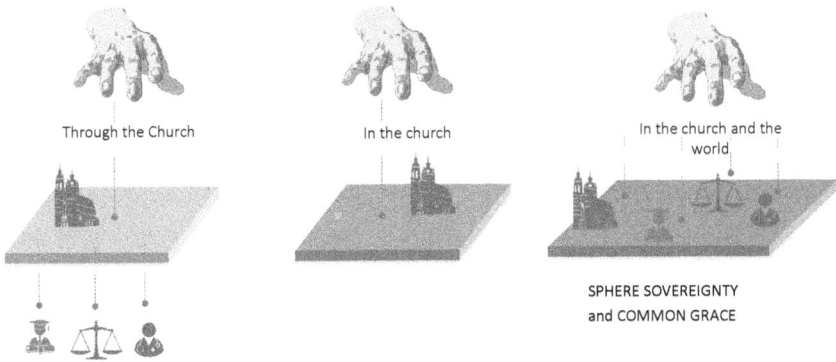

Figure 4.1

The final model is Kuyper's sphere sovereignty, whereby God is at work independently both in the church and in the world. Kuyper believed that God was sovereign in all spheres of life, and he famously wrote that "there is not a square inch in the whole domain of our human existence over which Christ, who is Sovereign over all, does not cry, Mine."[3] According to Kuyper, God's sovereignty is exercised in the world independently, in different spheres and unmediated by the church. This is why, for example, Kuyper founded the Free University of Amsterdam, which was to be free from the church and the state, and which would offer the goodness of education to the world under the direct influence of God's grace.

---

3. A. Kuyper, "Sphere Sovereignty," in *Abraham Kuyper: A Centennial Reader*, edited by James D. Bratt (Grand Rapids, MI: Eerdmans, 1998), 488.

The position taken in this chapter towards that which is secular adopts the model of sphere sovereignty and common grace and assumes that God is at work in the particular educational tradition of character and virtue education.

Prolegomenon 2: About Words

A second introductory matter deals with a handful of specialized words associated with character and virtue education. It is important to clarify our conceptual toolkit, both in order to avoid ambiguity and to prime the conversation for potential non-subject specific experts.

First, what is meant by *character education*? The word "character" is used today to mean a variety of things, including personality traits, emotional intelligence, leadership styles and learning styles. It is used in this chapter to mean none of these. The intended use draws on the millennial tradition of character education that has to do with the formational training of moral dispositions. This training is more than a prescription of rules and regulations as it aims at permanently shaping the moral outlook and general disposition of an individual. In short, character education, as we use it here, addresses the education of the sphere of moral being.

Furthermore, we are speaking of character and *virtue* education, and this raises the question of what is meant by "virtue."[4] The subject is vast, but the assumption here is that virtues have to do with dispositions that involve our entire being and make us think, want, feel, perceive and do that which is good. Many things can be said about the virtues. They are expressed in clusters, and we can construct taxonomies of virtues such as cardinal virtues, moral virtues, Christian virtues, civic virtues, intellectual virtues, and so on. Virtues operate in a number of significant and distinctive spheres of human life and can be private or public, material or immaterial, God-related, self-related, others-related or object-related. They are concerned with specific praiseworthy functioning and they are about being just, being prudent, being courageous, being temperate, being humble or being merciful. They are stable for, as Aristotle reminded us, one swallow does not make a spring. Virtue needs to be continuous in order to

---

4. The definition being used here is used widely by the Jubilee Centre for Character and Virtues: "Virtues constitute stable dispositional clusters concerned with praiseworthy functioning in a number of significant and distinctive spheres of human life" (J. Arthur et al., *Teaching Character and Virtue in Schools* [London: Routledge, 2017], 28).

constitute character. And, finally, virtues lead to human flourishing: character and virtue education assumes that we are created for virtue and that we reach our *telos* as human beings as we embody the virtues.

One might ask if it is permissible to use the more familiar term of *spiritual formation* as a synonym and substitute for character and virtue education. The brief answer is no.[5] Although there may be some overlap, spiritual formation is not the same thing for it has to do mainly with our relationship with God, whereas character and virtue education focuses on our moral growth. This distinction is educationally important, and we harm ourselves if we do not address this imprecision.[6]

That is not the only problem. As we think about the sacred-secular divide, it is unhelpful to privilege spiritual formation over character education, because it assumes a hierarchy where spirituality is more important and a dichotomy between religion and human flourishing that actually reinforces the sacred-secular divide rather than bridging it.

A Shared Tradition

We come now to the first part of the argument, which considers how character and virtue education can help bridge the sacred-secular divide as a shared tradition. There is much in common between the secular traditions of character and virtue and the Christian traditions, and this can represent a powerful point of contact. By means of a quick cavalcade across some of the main epochs of Western history we can learn from the fact that, over the centuries, the tradition of character and virtue education has been a lingua franca that has

---

5. For a scholarly discussion on this distinction, see D. Kelsey, "Reflections on a Discussion of Theological Education as Character Formation," *Theological Education* 25, no. 1 (1988), 62–75.

6. Ott comments on the possible disconnect between spirituality and character: "At first glance, it may seem the character development is a part of spirituality . . . We must, however, add what Paul Tournier once remarked, that especially among pious people, there would seem to be only a few who have a fully developed character. It is not given, apparently, that pious people are also mature people" (B. Ott, *Understanding and Developing Theological Education* [Carlisle: Langham Global Library, 2016], 225). Indeed, Lindbeck reminds us that "neurotics can be saints" (G. Lindbeck, "Spiritual Formation and Theological Education," *Theological Education*, Supplement 1 [1988]: 13).

been shared by philosophers and theologians alike. The examples that follow are only illustrative and selective.

Ancient Times

We can find many instances in ancient times of secular engagement with character and virtue. Central to Confucius's teaching in the *Analects*, for example, is the idea of *ren* as the perfect virtue.[7] The Mesopotamian collections of wisdom literature and epics such as *The Epic of Gilgamesh* are also replete with the concepts of character and virtue.[8] We can see the same recurrence in the "sacred" literature of the Old Testament, where we can find rich collections of ethical lists as well as heroic stories of virtue and vice. It can be argued that the wisdom books, such as Proverbs, are very close in their approach to the kind of virtue ethics that underlies character and virtue education, as we find that those who fear the Lord need not only to do good deeds, but to *be* people who are loving, trustworthy, humble, self-controlled, prudent, just, honest, kind, generous, truthful, gentle, patient, faithful, diligent, lovers of knowledge and zealous.

Classical Antiquity

Classical antiquity is probably the apex of the focus on character and virtue in Western culture, both in sacred and in secular environments. Any scholar of the classics will confirm that character and virtue are key concepts in Plato and Aristotle's vision of life and human nature,[9] and the practices of character and virtue form the core of both Greek *Paideia* and the Roman *virtus*-based education. Again and again, we find character and virtue as a common denominator in the teachings of Socrates, Plato, Aristotle, Seneca and Cicero as they lay the foundations of Western culture.

---

7. *Ren* could also be translated as "benevolence," "goodness" or "humanness" (S. Luo, "Confucius's Virtue Politics: Ren as Leadership Virtue," *Asian Philosophy* 22, no. 1 [Feb. 2012]: 15).

8. As Gilgamesh wonders, "there is moral growth: he learns, he changes" (T. Abusch, "The Development and Meaning of the Epic of Gilgamesh," *Journal of the American Oriental Society* 121, no. 4 [2001]: 615).

9. Plato's *The Republic*, for example, is often considered a great political treatise but in fact is an educational treatise on nurturing human nature in virtue to form the ideal state.

Although much debating went on in the early church concerning the relationship between philosophy and theology, those on the sacred side of the equation in classical antiquity exercised a profitable dialogue with the culture of character and virtue. Much could be written about how the New Testament itself provides evidence of this dialogue, in telling stories of heroes of virtue and providing ethical lists. Concerning the latter, for example, the New Testament features at least eight ethical lists of vices and fourteen ethical lists of virtues, the most notable being the Sermon on the Mount,[10] with as many identical virtues as those found on the secular lists.[11] The issue of the good moral life as an outworking of the gospel and as the source of deep happiness is also a key to reading many of the epistles[12] (certainly in Romans and James), and we find important concepts and words in the New Testament that are shared with the classical world, such as an andragogy of imitation, the vision of wisdom as discernment in doing good, or specific words like *arête*[13] and *dikaiosune*.[14]

In this period, the early church also engaged with their secular counterpart around character and virtue. The desert fathers and mothers, for example, grounded their mystical vision with control over the passions of vice which

---

10. See, for example, N. T. Wright on the links between the Beatitudes and virtue (N. T. Wright, *After You Believe* [New York: Harper Collins, 2010], 103–108). The Beatitudes, he claims, could be mistaken for a list of rules, but they are much more like virtues.

11. It is beyond the scope of this chapter to detail the differences between the classical tradition of character and virtue education and the vision that emerges from the New Testament. Clearly they are not identical, and important differences arise, such as the appearance in some ethical lists such as the Sermon on the Mount of virtues such as forgiveness, love and modesty that were relatively foreign to the assertive classical world. And yet "many scholars have claimed that in cataloguing these 'virtues' Paul has taken over 'a current list from a textbook of ethical instruction, and made it his own,' using the material in much the same way as pagan moral philosophers of his day when instructing their adherents" (Peter O'Brien, *The Epistle to the Philippians: A Commentary on the Greek Text*, The New International Greek Testament Commentary [Grand Rapids, MI: Eerdmans, 1991], 501).

12. See, for example, the commentary on Phil 4:8–9 in O'Brien, *Epistle to the Philippians*.

13. This is a key word in Greek philosophy that describes virtue. It is used by Paul in Phil 4:8 to summarize an ethical list and by Peter in 2 Pet 1 as a key component of the life of faith.

14. Aristotle, for example, reinterpreted *dikaiosune* into *arête*, using the two terms as broad synonyms. But for Plato, *dikaousune* was the "allocation of each part of the soul to its particular function, and no other" (A. MacIntyre, *After Virtue* [London: Duckworth, 2007], 141).

begins the road to holiness, virtue and union with God.[15] Origen's teachings are full of references to virtue,[16] as are Cassian's.[17] Augustine also engages deeply with the tradition of character and virtue in *The City of God*, and Ambrose purposely mimics Cicero's *De Officis* as he sets out the way of character and virtue in the training of church priests.

The Middle Ages

In the Middle Ages, philosophy is dominated by Aristotle and we see a proliferation of literature around the virtues, the most famous probably being Dante's *Divine Comedy* in which heaven, hell and purgatory themselves are arranged around the vices and virtues. Politics is also deeply saturated by this vision, as illustrated, for example, by Lorenzetti's frescoes in *The Palazzo dei Governatori* of Siena, where he depicts a fantastic vision of virtue and its effects on government, leading to well-being, beauty, industry, education, leisure, arts,

---

15. John the Dwarf provides an example of an ethical list: "I think it best that a man should have a little bit of all the virtues. Therefore, get up early every day and acquire the beginning of every virtue and every commandment of God. Use great patience, with fear and long-suffering, in the love of God, with all the fervour of your soul and body. Exercise great humility, bear with interior distress; be vigilant and pray often with reverence and groaning, with purity of speech and control of your eyes. When you are despised do not get angry; be at peace, and do not render evil for evil. Do not pay attention to the faults of others, and do not try to compare yourself with others, knowing you are less than every created thing. Renounce everything material and that which is of the flesh. Live by the cross, in warfare, in poverty of spirit, in voluntary spiritual asceticism, in fasting, penitence and tears, in discernment, in purity of soul, taking hold of that which is good. Do your work in peace. Persevere in keeping vigil, in hunger and thirst, in cold and nakedness, and in sufferings. Shut yourself in a tomb as though you were already dead, so that at all times you will think death is near" (quoted in B. Ward, *The Sayings of the Desert Fathers* [Kalamazoo, MI: Cicercian, 1975], 92).

16. "The teachers of Alexandria mostly were not interested in conveying knowledge or transmitting intellectual skills. They were interested in moral and spiritual formation" (R. J. Neuhaus, *Theological Education and Moral Formation* [Grand Rapids, MI: Eerdmans, 1992], 42).

17. Cassian mentions a "tree of virtue" in the *Institutis*, indicating that pride is the vice that will most easily attack those who are closest to achieving all the other virtues. "There is then no other fault which is so destructive of all virtues, and robs and despoils a man of all righteousness and holiness, as this evil of pride, which like some pestilential disease attacks the whole man, and, not content to damage one part or one limb only, injures the entire body by its deadly influence, and endeavours to cast down by a most fatal fall, and destroy those who were already at the top of the tree of the virtue" (*Institutis* 12.3). "It generally attacks those only who have conquered the former faults and have already almost arrived at the top of the tree in respect of the virtues" (*Institutis* 24).

safety, prosperity and peaceful cohabitation, all counterbalanced by a horrific vision of the effects of governments full of vice on city and the countryside.

On the "sacred" side of the conversation, we find that the monastic movement is placing a recurring emphasis on virtue, with St Benedict's and St Francis's rules perhaps being the most notorious instances. Several great theologians are also seen to be grappling with virtue and vice. Abelard, for example, wrestled with the classical tradition of pagan philosophers and safely relied on Cicero, arguing that ancient philosophers were able to write effectively about the virtues because they were virtuous people themselves, and pointing to a long tradition of Christian writers, including Augustine, Alcuin and Ambrose, who engaged fruitfully with the classical writings on the virtues. Aquinas is clearly the *sacred* giant in this period, and he engages extensively with virtue, taking much space in the *Prima* and *Secunda Secundae* of his *Summa Theologiae* to provide a definitive contribution to the theology of character and virtue.[18]

The Renaissance and Modernity

There is no space to fully explore the tradition of character and virtue in the Renaissance and in modernity, but it can be noted that the major philosophers of this period all engaged significantly with this tradition. Among them we can safely list Locke, Hume, Kant, Marx, Tocqueville and Emerson. John Locke, for example, in writing his highly influential *Some Thoughts Concerning Education*, claimed that the most important goal of education was to create the virtuous man. On the other side of the divide the dialogue over this tradition continued, and we find Christian theologians, educators and founders of ecclesial movements deeply engaged with issues of character and virtue. We can list, for example, noted individuals like à Kempis, Comenius, Spener and the founders of the Jesuit movement. We also find Melanchthon, the educationalist in the Reformation, who believed that all levels of education should "not only study the subject matter at hand but also create virtue."[19]

---

18. See chapter 47 of the *Summa*, which is particularly rich in references to the virtues.
19. Quoted in P. Sheldrake, *A Brief History of Spirituality* (Oxford: Blackwell, 2007), 72.

Today

As we come to the present, there are remarkable developments on the secular side of the equation where a renaissance in the rediscovery of the value of character and virtue in society can be seen. Nobel prizes are offered for the virtues of justice, generosity, compassion and peace, and good character is seen as essential in diminishing crime rates. Virtue is appearing in scholarly studies as a factor that limits materialism in society, and the world of work recognizes that non-virtuous business practices lead to increasing entropy, disorder and inefficiency. Virtue is increasingly pointed to as that which is good for society, beneficial to health, enhancing of law practices and fundamental for democracy. In education there is a veritable revival of neo-Aristotelian virtue ethics and it is increasingly frequent to find character and virtue education programs in many schools and state educational policies.

But what is happening in the church and in theological education today? As the world reconsiders virtue, it seems that the church has lost a vocabulary of virtue as it shies away from moralism through fear of appearing legalistic, cultish and unaccepting. An uncritical captivity to the paradigms of situationism have also weakened the churches' stand on that which is good. This is not just hesitancy in the face of difficult moral dilemmas over abortion, pacifism or human sexuality, but a more generic reluctance to make explicit commitments even to general virtues. An exploration of recent publications in evangelical discipleship manuals, for example, reveals that many models of discipleship rarely feature direct reference to character and virtue.

Likewise, in theological education, little is delivered at degree program levels that makes character and virtue education clear, central and intentional. In discontinuity with the previous epochs, the "sacred" side of the conversation over character and virtue seems to have gone relatively silent both in the church and in the theological academy. Perhaps theological educators wonder (as does Stanley Fish[20]) whether character and virtue education falls within their remit, and they choose to "aim low" and consider only the objectives of professional and academic education. Perhaps theological educators are not sure about how assessment or accreditation might work out, and struggle to

---

20. This debate is found in E. Kiss and P. Euben, *Debating Moral Education* (Durham/London: Duke University Press, 2010).

design learning outcomes and curricula that include character and virtue. Or perhaps theological educators are simply caught up in the perpetuation of the familiar post-Enlightenment educational paradigms that have little curricular space for formational objectives.

Whatever the case, theological education seems to have slipped off the shoulders of the giants and, despite its heritage and unique potential, it is shying away from the discourse and the practice of virtue. In doing so, it not only impoverishes its contribution to the lives of its graduates, but also forfeits a natural bridge into the secular. To the degree that the conversation between secular society and educational philosophies and theological education over character and virtue education is not happening, we will miss a natural opportunity of sacred-secular dialogue.

A Shared Objective

In the second section of this chapter we consider character and virtue education as a shared objective that can bring together the sacred and the secular. This is looking not so much to the past as to the present and to the future. In particular, we will look at how theological education can be used to train graduates who fulfil a kind of *missio Dei* that strongly resonates with the needs and desires of society. There is a shared song sheet to be found in the objectives of character and virtue education that both sacred and secular communities can sing from.

The "Cape Town Commitment" reminded the evangelical world that its *missio Dei* was more than evangelism and church planting; it included a mission to improve society. In the Commitment it is stated that we "bear witness to Jesus Christ . . . in every sphere of society, and in the realm of ideas" . . . and that "integral mission means discerning, proclaiming, and living out, the biblical truth that the gospel is God's good news . . . for society."[21]

These three objectives can be unpacked as an agenda for dialogue between theological education and secular society around character and virtue.

---

21. Drawn from "Cape Town Commitment," https://www.lausanne.org/content/ctcommitment#capetown, Foreword and Section 7.

Sharing Ideas

Christians need to bear witness to Jesus Christ in the realm of specific ideas around what it means to be a good person and how to become one. This is something that society is interested in. It is looking to philosophy to tell it what virtue is and to education to help it nourish goodness. Does theological education have a contribution to offer in this quest? Does theology have ideas about virtue? Can education done around the discipline of theology develop and share ideas with the broader society on what kind of formational practices will intentionally shape character and foster virtue? Should Christian theological educators not be publishing in the journals about this, and joining the choir of ideas and voices in the search for the good?

These questions carry affirmative answers and the Christian faith is uniquely poised to build on the tradition of character and virtue education through a deep inner transformation that goes beyond educational technique, wise teaching and motivational drive. Indeed, the idea we have to share is that Jesus Christ has come to give us the power to become the virtuous kinds of people that Aristotle dreamed of and that society is looking for today.

Impacting Society

When we speak of impacting society and culture, much will depend on the position taken in Niebuhr's *Christ and Culture* debate. We are here assuming the "Christ converts culture" model, where the Christian task includes working with Christ to convert and transform culture.

As we think about theological education and character and virtue education, there is before us an opportunity to impact culture at the most fundamental level by shaping virtuous character in individuals. The problems of society and culture are not organizational, nor are they due to the lack of laws and regulations. The problems of society start at the level of individual character and it is there that theological education can make a difference. As this happens, theological educators join hands with the secular in a shared objective. In the previous section we saw how society has rediscovered the value of character and virtue. Society wants a culture of justice, equity, peace and order. UNESCO, for example, looks at the global emergencies of population growth, pollution, global warming and energy supplies, and claims that the response is found in a greater moral framework in higher education.[22] The deepest felt needs of the world are met through women and men of virtue, and theological education stands as a powerful global contributor.

> As graduates of virtue and character exit from a programme of theological education, they bless society by being good citizens and bringing general benefits overall. More virtue will strengthen social bonds of solidarity. It will reduce crime and delinquency. It will effectively combat corruption and increase productivity. It will increase justice and reduce the need for punitive justice. It will improve democracy, for if you give power to good people, you are likely to have good outcomes for everyone . . . Theological education is strategically positioned across the planet to provide a robust injection of virtuous citizens into society. This is not only a good in itself but can be a powerful apologetic of the relevance of the Christian faith.[23]

Being Good News

Let's face it, secular society does not have a high view of theological education, nor does it see much use for the discipline of theology. Although a much broader argument is needed to respond to this misplaced perception, one starting argument for the relevance of theological education lies in its unique ability to inject virtuous citizens into society. This can also become a powerful apologetic of the relevance of the Christian faith. As rationalism has weakened its grasp and the bite of postmodernism has diminished the traction of classical and propositional apologetics, *being good news* in contributing virtuous citizens to society may represent a new approach to apologetics.

In this new apologetic, theological education has a critical role to play, for there is no better breeding ground for character and virtue than in a theological school. Theological education, in fact, deals with consenting adults. It deals

22. See *Report on the World Conference on Higher Education* (UNESCO, 1998), https://unesdoc.unesco.org/ark:/48223/pf0000113664?posInSet=2&queryId=28942914-f30a-42df-bf44-bd3e3fda9e0f, accessed 26 October 2020.
23. M. Oxenham, *Character and Virtue in Theological Education* (Carlisle: Langham Global Library, 2019), 18.

with future leaders. It deals with those who have a transforming Spirit who is at work in them. It deals with those who are highly motivated and morally keen. It deals with students over a sufficiently prolonged period of time to empower habitation practices. It deals with a naturally connected subject matter (theology) and sits on a giant tradition that will allow seamless integration of virtue-related objectives. It deals with those going into kinds of employment where character and virtue are demanded, and it deals with stakeholders who value virtue. No other societal institution offers such a unique combination.

This chapter argues that character and virtue education can contribute a fresh line of deed-based apologetic strategy through theological education. As Christian theological education contributes women and men of character and virtue to society, it bears a significant testimony to the relevance of Christianity.

Conclusion

It is 1610, and Michelangelo Merisi, also known as Caravaggio, is on the run after having killed a man in the alleys of Rome. As part of his plea for mercy to Paul V, Caravaggio offers a painting of *David and Goliath*. This is probably his last painting as he will die of fever shortly thereafter on his return voyage to Rome. He has painted the story of David and Goliath before, but this time it is different. It is autobiographical, and it signals a deep change in character. The image of Goliath's head, with its eyes still open and mouth gaping, is in fact a self-portrait of Caravaggio. On the blade of Goliath's sword in David's hand, one can make out the inscription *HASOS*. This is an acronym of the Augustinian motto *humilitas occidit superbiam*: "humility conquers pride." This is Caravaggio's final painting, and his final message to the world: "After a life of pride, humility has conquered me."

Today, theological education all over the world is suffering from a Philistine domination of academics, of scientific critical thinking, of the measurement paradigms in accreditation, of the efficiency traps of professionalization and of the pride of achievement and ranking. As we've served Goliath, we ourselves have become like Goliath, and in this time of slavery Christian theological education struggles to find a place for that which is at its heart: holistic formation of Kingdom humans.

But not all of Goliath's armour is bad. His sword is a good sword. It bears the mark of humility, which is the starting virtue in the formation of character and virtue. It is time to pick up this sword and cut off the proud head of where we may have gone wrong. May humility conquer pride and open a new season of Kingdom work.

Questions for Personal Reflection and Group Discussion

1. Take a moment to reflect upon the three models the author mentions that describe ways in which God's common grace is at work in the world: (a) through the church; (b) in the church; (c) in the church and the world/sphere sovereignty. Which of these understandings of common grace have been most present in your own assumptions, and in those of your theological institution and faith tradition?

2. In your own context, how do these assumptions regarding common grace influence the ways in which Christians interpret the world and relate to secular society? Discuss personal examples, and examples that are representative of your seminary and church context.

3. Discuss ways in which the curriculum of your institution addresses the formation of character and virtue, as defined by the author. Evaluate existing curricular and co-curricular strategies of character and virtue development in your theological institution. Is this a strength of your institution? How can it be further focused and strengthened in the seminary curriculum?

4. Reflect upon your own faith tradition and that of other evangelical churches in your context. To what degree is character and virtue formation present in commonly held understandings and practices of discipleship? What suggestions can you offer to strengthen Christian moral and ethical development through the teaching and discipleship ministries of the local church? In what place in your teaching can you explore and encourage these ideas with your students?

5. Reflect upon and evaluate the author's affirmation that character and virtue education constitutes a shared objective for both sacred and secular communities and as such forms a key part of integral mission.

6. Pause and pray for some of the local secular communities and institutions.

7. With regards to the proposed "agenda for dialogue between theological education and secular society around character and virtue," how might this look in practice? Share examples of churches and theological institutions in your context that have been effective in fulfilling the triple objective of sharing ideas, impacting society and being good news.

8. Discuss practical ways in which these same objectives might be fulfilled to a greater degree through your own teaching ministry, theological institution and church context.

9. Pause and pray for your institutional engagement with character development ideas and practice.

References

Abusch, T. "The Development and Meaning of the Epic of Gilgamesh." *Journal of the American Oriental Society* 121, no. 4 (2001): 614–622.

Arthur, J., et al. *Teaching Character and Virtue in Schools*. London: Routledge, 2017.

Johnson, G. P. "The Myth of Common Grace." *The Trinity Review*, March/April 1987. Accessed 27 November 2018. http://trinityfoundation.org/PDF/The%20 Trinity%20Review%200055a%20TheMythofCommonGrace.pdf.

Kelsey, D. "Reflections on a Discussion of Theological Education as Character Formation." *Theological Education* 25, no. 1 (1988): 62–75.

Kiss, E., and P. Euben. *Debating Moral Education*. Durham/London: Duke University Press, 2010.

Kuyper, A. *Common Grace: God's Gifts for a Fallen World*. Ashland: Lexham Press, 2015.

———. "Sphere Sovereignty." In *Abraham Kuyper: A Centennial Reader*, edited by James D. Bratt, 461–490. Grand Rapids, MI: Eerdmans, 1998.

Lindbeck, G. "Spiritual Formation and Theological Education." *Theological Education*, Supplement 1 (1988): 10–23.

Luo, S. "Confucius's Virtue Politics: Ren as Leadership Virtue." *Asian Philosophy* 22, no. 1 (Feb. 2012): 15–35.

MacIntyre, A. *After Virtue*. London: Duckworth, 2007.

Mouw, Richard, J. "Some Reflections on Sphere Sovereignty." In *Religion, Pluralism and Public Life: Abraham Kuyper's Legacy for the Twenty-First Century*, edited by Luis E. Lugo, 160–182. Grand Rapids, MI: Eerdmans, 2000.

Neuhaus, R. J. *Theological Education and Moral Formation.* Grand Rapids, MI: Eerdmans, 1992.

O'Brien, Peter. *The Epistle to the Philippians: A Commentary on the Greek Text.* The New International Greek Testament Commentary. Grand Rapids, MI: Eerdmans, 1991.

Ott, B. *Understanding and Developing Theological Education.* Carlisle: Langham Global Library, 2016.

Oxenham, M. *Character and Virtue in Theological Education.* Carlisle: Langham Global Library, 2019.

Sheldrake, P. *A Brief History of Spirituality.* Oxford: Blackwell, 2007.

Ward, B. *The Sayings of the Desert Fathers.* Kalamazoo, MI: Cicercian, 1975.

Wright, N. T. *After You Believe.* New York: Harper Collins, 2010.

5

Pastoral Identity Formation within Theological Education

Marilyn Naidoo

What changes a person from someone merely knowledgeable about the Bible, church practice and pastoral care to an actual pastor? To someone who is a leader, secure in personal identity, acting with appropriate authority, and living out the vocation with passion and integrity? The making of the pastor requires some reflection on integrating theory and practice, skill and wisdom, and being and doing emanating from a secure pastoral identity. This chapter highlights that the theological training experience is a critical time to develop self-awareness in students, so that students can strengthen the fragile disparate aspects of themselves and their role in regard to their various circles of accountability and ministry. This work is known as identity formation which involves the student and seminary community processes.

To avoid confusion and to understand the interplay, it is important to note that identity formation falls within the broad area of ministerial or pastoral formation. Ministerial formation is the umbrella concept. It is a multifaceted activity involving critical thinking, the acquisition of knowledge, pastoral skills development and religious identity formation, together with the development of the spiritual maturity expected of church ministers.[1] Formative practices engage the whole person and do not simply isolate the spiritual, intellectual or professional aspects of the person's life. Evangelicals, on the other hand, refer to this broad concept of development as "spiritual formation," a somewhat vague[2] assortment of individuals, emphases and practices that deals with the nature and dynamics of growth in Christian holiness. However, in mainline Protestant and Catholic traditions,[3] spiritual formation is viewed as only one part of formation and only concerns a person's spiritual relationship with God. In this chapter I take this latter view, so identity formation is only one part of the complex work of ministerial formation. Ministerial or pastoral formation is about "ongoing development of identity of moving toward what may be referred to as their greater authenticity, more authentic identity and authenticity vocation."[4] Integrity in ministry requires continuing reflection on life and vocation so that ministers can be, as Parker Palmer says, "at home in their own souls."[5] To be at home in one's soul, one must know who one is, how one is shaped and formed, what values and prejudices one still harbours, and what one believes about those different from oneself. Here identity formation is developed around the idea of authenticity, which speaks to developing inner coherence within the person.

Christian leadership is not about the external trappings and privileges of the office but the profound sense of identity that comes from conforming oneself as a servant of the gospel. For some this "boils down pragmatically

---

1. Marilyn Naidoo, "Ministerial Formation and Practical Theology," *International Journal of Practical Theology* 19, no. 1 (2015): 1–25.

2. "Vague" because of the absence of a widely recognized and unified system of spiritual practice; it is left to individual expositors and believers to relate the biblical principles to the practicalities of daily life in a modern world. This produces a wide and often contradictory variety of interpretations and is confusing to those trying to understand biblical teaching and to practise evangelical spirituality. See David Parker, "Evangelical Spirituality Reviewed," *The Evangelical Quarterly* 63, no. 2 (1991): 123–148.

3. Joretta Marshall, "Formative Practices: Intent, Structure, and Content," *Reflective Practice: Formation and Supervision in Ministry* 29 (2009): 56–72.

4. Parker Palmer, *The Courage to Teach: Exploring the Inner Landscape of a Teacher's Life* (San Francisco: Jossey-Bass, 2007), 50.

5. Palmer, *Courage to Teach*, 56.

to learning what a minister should do, a well-constructed self-image."[6] It is a formula-driven approach to ministry driven by one's agendas. Considering the personal dysfunction in ministry, the lack of relational skills and the rise in clergy misconduct, the tendency to hide parts of the true self has implications for public ministry. Leadership in general is full of temptations and gives ample opportunity for various kinds of abuse.[7] Self-deception, as well as the deception of others, misuse of time and resources, manipulation of others by means of one's professional knowledge and power, and other forms of depravity are possible.

Theological education needs to provide strong foundations for pastoral identity, so that future pastors can make discerning judgments based on well-formulated understandings rather than on "quick-fix" solutions.[8] Many theological institutions have been passive and unsure about how to develop formational education.[9] It is thus important to understand the outworkings of identity formation, as this awareness can help theological educators in the formation process to help students determine their social role as "pastor" or "missionary" and successfully integrate their professional selves into their multiple identities, so that they act from a place of authenticity.

The Secular-Sacred Divide

The concept of identity development cannot be understood without understanding the human person and human psychology. As we draw connections between the focus of nurturing inner coherence and the secular-sacred divide we need to note two significant challenges in this regard: our theological understanding of the human person, and our understanding of

---

6. James R. Estep and Jonathan H. Kim, *Christian Formation: Integrating Theology and Human Development* (Nashville: B&H, 2010), 23.

7. Virginia S. Cetuk, *What to Expect in Seminary: Theological Education as Spiritual Formation* (Nashville: Abingdon, 1998), 45.

8. Gregory Jones and Kevin Armstrong, *Resurrecting Excellence: Shaping Faithful Christian Ministry* (Grand Rapids, MI: Eerdmans, 2006), 6.

9. See Walter Liefeld and Linda Cannell, "Spiritual Formation and Theological Education," in *Alive to God: Studies in Spirituality*, ed. J. I. Packer and Loren Wilkinson (Downers Grove, IL: InterVarsity Press, 1992), 239–252, for a discussion on the various studies done in Protestant seminaries in the United States, as an example.

vocation. If these issues are embraced it can narrow the secular-sacred divide and can help shape attempts at formation in a more meaningful way.

First, we affirm that Christianity is committed to the secular because of creation and the incarnation. It is important to note that in understanding the inner life, the doctrine of salvation has been emphasized at the expense of the doctrine of creation. This move has left evangelical efforts at formation operating without sufficiently nuanced understandings of human creatureliness, embodiment or sociality. This dichotomy reflects the Platonic approach[10] that describes the human person as dualistic, composed of spirit and body. The fundamental distinction between the material and the physical, between the soul and the body, and between the inner life of spiritual reality and the outer life of the everyday, has been problematic. Evangelical Christianity has been criticized for its persistent other-worldliness[11] which refuses to take this life seriously, and "confuses the 'flesh' (sarx) with the 'body' (soma), as if anything material were intrinsically evil and the body could not become the temple of the Holy Spirit."[12]

Ministerial formation, including identity formation, is human as it deals with the human development process because this is where we live and what we live from. As creatures fashioned by God, our identities are a mix of our genetic make-up, our family history, culture and upbringing, our experiences – all that has gone into making us unique persons. In our humanness we are constructed holistically with a wholeness and completeness that does not allow us to be divided into this or that part. We are human beings in our entirety, image bearers of God, and have "special standing" in creation.[13] The classical doctrine of the *imago Dei* suggests human beings are equipped with intellect and will, abilities and desires to know and to realize their potential as much as possible in the context of embodied, ordinary life. In an age of depersonalization, we need a theological anthropology that is grounded in the humanity of Jesus Christ (i.e. the christological focus of the *imago Dei*) that fundamentally orients

---

10. Rodney Starke and Roger Finke, *Acts of Faith: Explaining the Human Side of Religion* (Berkeley, CA: University of California Press, 2000), 112.

11. Mark A. Noll, *Between Faith and Criticism* (Vancouver: Regent College Pub., 2004), 6.

12. Parker, "Evangelical Spirituality," 126.

13. Stanley J. Grenz, *Theology for the Community of God* (Grand Rapids, MI: Eerdmans, 1994), 177–180.

and reorients what it means to be fully and truly human.[14] It is important to note that the humanity of Christ (Col 2:9–10) relates the sacred to the secular by transforming humanity and repositioning it within the world. The work of Christ came to rehabilitate his image in *all* persons. Thus, we participate in the full humanity of Christ as the source and growth of our own humanity, bringing together the sacred and secular in communities.

For too long we have had the assumed anthropology of persons as *thinking beings*. The assumption is that if a person thinks correctly, he or she will act correctly. However, ministerial training then involves more than teaching students a particular way of thinking; it requires those ways of thinking to be linked constructively with ways of being and doing. Smith, using cognitive neuroscience and social psychology, argues that humans, at their core, primarily are not thinking beings but are "liturgical animals."[15] His argument is that anthropology is "deeply embodied in the actual physicality of human personhood and embedded in the social context of human relatedness."[16] In this regard we know the Bible affirms the material world as created by God; it reminds us that Jesus had a body and does still; and promises that eternal life includes a new body and involves a new earth, as well as new heavens. This knowledge should influence our understanding of our very humanity. This in no way diminishes the involvement of the Holy Spirit, but acknowledges that humanity was created to be in relationship with God. The secular-sacred divide, however, makes people believe that art, music and the many ways in which human beings express their God-given human creativity have no place in the kingdom of God – unless they have overtly biblical themes.[17] Similarly, the secular-sacred divide leads to a negative view of the body, and of physical pleasures.

Part of the challenge in living out this integrated focus to spiritual transformation may be because of spiritual impatience in the long journey of transformation, a tendency made worse by the pressures of a culture of

---

14. Estep and Kim, *Christian Formation*, 35.

15. James K. A. Smith, *Desiring the Kingdom: Worship Worldview and Cultural Formation* (Grand Rapids, MI: Baker Academic, 2009), 65.

16. Smith, *Desiring the Kingdom*, 69.

17. Nancy R. Pearcey, *Total Truth: Liberating Christianity from Its Cultural Captivity* (Wheaton, IL: Crossway, 2004), 67.

relentless hyperactivity. When blended with our culture's thoroughgoing pragmatism, it can devolve into a lazy anti-intellectualism that seeks little beyond a handful of pre-packaged "simple steps to spiritual success" which are nothing more than a bare-bones instrumental rationality focusing on "right behaviour."[18] In addition, because spiritual formation remains firmly rooted in Scripture as the sole authority in matters of faith and practice, extra-biblical sources such as insights regarding spiritual maturation in psychology, church history, subjective experience and philosophy would seem to encourage practices and principles that are not explicitly endorsed by the biblical text (e.g. spiritual direction, journaling, silent retreats) instead of focusing on normative biblical principles of growth. However, according to Porter, what should be our ultimate concern is whether the principle or practice can be affirmed from God's general and special revelation.[19]

Second, in making links to the secular-sacred, the concept of vocation is central. When Christian leaders and pastors speak of reasons for embracing ministry, they inevitably include an aspect of divine "call" which means "called out" from ordinary work to full-time ministry – in other words, it is not a general call to any possible ministry. "Vocation" is from the Latin word for calling, constructed as something that is individual, deeply personal, a unique experience and essential for ordination. But for all that, the fact remains that we frequently *do* unreflectively embody the sacred-secular divide. John Stott's essay titled "Guidance, Vocation and Ministry"[20] is helpful as it underlines that God's general will for all Christians is that they grow in Christlikeness. Stott explains that God has a particular will for each Christian, which is his or her "vocation." In the biblical usage of "vocation," Stott observes, the "emphasis is not on the human (what we do) but on the divine (what *God* has called us to do)."

---

18. Given this understanding of the Christian life, if the believer fails in his or her endeavour (as he or she no doubt will), the only help on offer is an exhortation to confess, repent and try harder the next time. See John Coe's analysis of this in "Resisting the Temptation of Moral Formation: Opening to Spiritual Formation in the Cross and Spirit," *Journal of Spiritual Formation and Soul Care* 1, no. 1 (2008): 54–78.

19. Steve L. Porter, "Sanctification in a New Key: Relieving Evangelical Anxieties over Spiritual Formation," *Journal of Spiritual Formation and Soul Care* 1, no. 2 (2008): 129–148.

20. In John Stott, *The Contemporary Christian* (Downers Grove, IL: InterVarsity Press, 1992), 128–140.

What we must notice is that our individual callings are whatever God would have each of us do toward fulfilling the cultural mandate and the Great Commission. This realization is what prompted the Reformer Martin Luther to insist that "tailors, cobblers, stonemasons, carpenters, cooks, innkeepers, farmers and all the temporal craftsmen have been 'consecrated' to the work and office of [their] trade" just as pastors have been to their office.[21] Luther recognized that when we use the word "calling" correctly, there is no room left for thinking that only certain jobs are sacred, whereas others are secular. Vinoth Ramachandra suggests that theologians need to "help artists, economists, doctors and other professionals to think through in Christian perspective their 'secular' callings."[22] Yet theological education tends to empower only an elite, and not all the people of God. An individual who experiences a divine call "upon his/her life" serves God "as a spiritual leader." And we have the divide between those who serve in full-time and "secular" positions. By demolishing this dichotomy, we realize that God cares about all the work we do.[23] The innermost core of the person deals with beliefs, identity and mission, and highly personal questions as to what end the pastor or Christian worker wants to work, or even what he or she sees as his or her personal calling in the world. The question deals with what is deep inside that moves us to do what we do.

The secular-sacred divide brings into direct focus these two issues of human personhood and vocation which are both deeply tied to the concept of identity. This chapter offers a model of identity formation that forms theological students on a corporate and individual level. If theological educators can deepen their awareness of how identity is being shaped in seminaries, this awareness can bring about new practices which can then close this gap between the secular and the sacred.

---

21. Quoted in Richard T. Hughes, *The Vocation of a Christian Scholar: How Christian Faith Can Sustain the Life of the Mind* (Grand Rapids, MI: Eerdmans, 2005), 45.

22. Howard Peskett and Vinoth Ramachandra, *The Message of Mission* (Bangalore: SAIACS Press, 2003), 35.

23. George M. Marsden, *Evangelicalism and Modern America* (Grand Rapids, MI: Eerdmans, 1984), xiv.

Identity Formation

The unique characteristic of the pastoral profession involves the identity of the pastor, which applies to the person, and the competence of the pastor, which, in turn, impacts on the profession. Identity refers to a sense of personal wholeness, and there are distinctions between personal identity, pastoral identity and theological identity.[24] Two questions are important in this connection: "Who am I?" and "What am I supposed to do?" Heitink cautions that one must realize that the three states of existence – being simultaneously a pastor, a believer and a human being – constantly interact as stimuli, while external factors of a social or theological nature may add to the crisis.[25]

Identity then is a complex construct: a continuous forming and reforming of the person. It is "multiple, dynamic, relational, situated, embedded in relations of power, yet negotiable."[26] Erikson's[27] classic model sees identity as an inner unity that is destabilized through developmental conflicts, whereas Parker Palmer[28] views identity as an "evolving nexus where all forces converge in the mystery of self." In *Educating Clergy*, Charles Foster and colleagues[29] argue that formation is at the centre of educating clergy because compared to other professions, the training of clergy is particularly concerned with "meaning, purpose and identity." Educating clergy, they assert, should involve far more than cognitive knowledge, for its primary aim is to enable the student to become a person who thinks, feels and acts a certain way.

It is important to note that students are always being shaped and formed inside and outside education, whether it is intentional or not. Theology educators assume that persons have been shaped and formed in the context of the local church and have developed their spirituality before arriving at seminary, but this may not be the case. What is true is that students who end up in seminary arrive already formed by a variety of life experiences and

24. Gerben Heitink, *Practical Theology: History, Theory, Action Domains – Manual for Practical Theology* (Grand Rapids, MI: Eerdmans, 1993), 311.

25. Heitink, *Practical Theology*, 312.

26. Steph Lawler, *Identity: Sociological Perspectives* (Cambridge: Polity, 2008), 45.

27. Erik H. Erickson, *Identity: Youth and Crisis* (New York: Norton, 1968).

28. Palmer, *Courage to Teach*, 13.

29. Charles Foster, Lisa Dahill, Larry Golemon and Barbara Tolentino, *Educating Clergy: Teaching Practices and Pastoral Imaginations* (San Francisco: Jossey-Bass, 2006), 101.

popular culture, and have internalized views on theology, church traditions, race, social and economic class, religious diversity, and the like. Students assume theological institutions will help integrate their spirituality, character and personal struggles, and are often disappointed to discover that theological education has not helped them in this regard.

As theological students transition from theological studies to the world of congregational ministry, very little attention is paid to how students construct a public persona of being a pastor or how they develop inner coherence. The integration of learning is left as a responsibility for the student with little reflection on identity and formation issues. Students can experience considerable anxiety or depression in the first years of ministry. They can struggle to differentiate between personal identity and pastoral identity. Their understanding of self and nurturing appropriate relationships in relation to their vocational call is not so clear. Hence students are entitled to ask: How does my identity as a young black African woman from a theologically conservative evangelical tradition shape how I see the world and act in Christian ministry? How is my identity and gender received in my church context, and is there enough space to be myself? In my context of South Africa, with its oppressive political history and the psychological scaring of racism, working out identity issues is the start of authentic Christian ministry.[30] Students need to work through their own personal concerns and inner coherence from which they act out. This is because identity encompasses how people understand themselves, how they interpret their experiences, how they present themselves and wish to be perceived by others, and how they are recognized by the broader community. If people have not come to terms with who they are as individuals, then no amount of preparation will help. Instead it will underline their inadequacy and lack of proper place.

---

30. Marilyn Naidoo, "An Empirical Study on Spiritual Formation at Theological Training Institutions in South Africa," *Religion and Theology* 18, no. 4 (2011): 118–146.

A Model of Identity Formation

It is important to note that identity is formed through individual cognition *and* through sociocultural processes which construct knowledge.[31] Due to limitations of space, I briefly mention the Personality and Social Structure Perspective (PSSP) of identity formation[32] which is a useful framework for better understanding the difficulties and complexities of identity formation. The PSSP model "conceptualizes the processes underlying the development of students' professional identity in two ways":[33]

1. At the collective level, which involves a socialization of the person into appropriate roles and forms of participation in the environment;
2. At the level of the individual, which involves the psychological development of the person, and engages pedagogical and methodological interventions.

Collective Level

Identity formation is mainly social and relational in nature and is heavily influenced by the institution and broader social-economic-political environment. Within the social structure or institutional culture, there are regulated ways in which people relate and organize social life – the unwritten rules. Newcomers to the group are expected to learn what is acceptable to the group by observing the behaviour of the group and adapting accordingly.

In the social structure there are systems of recognitions and misrecognitions along the fault lines of race, gender, sexuality, class, ethnicity, and so on. "One way regulatory power works is by categorizing people in terms through which they come to understand themselves."[34] Identities are shaped by the perceptions of the spaces they occupy. People become subjected to the rules and norms engendered by knowledge about these identities. For example, as a woman I am expected to act in a certain way and come to understand my identity accordingly. These identities are learnt and are an outcome of social practices.

---

31. Lawler, *Identity*, 34.
32. James S. House, "The Three Faces of Social Psychology," *Sociometry* 40, no. 2 (1977): 161–177.
33. James E. Cote and Charles G. Levine, *Identity, Formation, Agency and Culture* (Mahwah, NJ: Lawrence Erlbaum Associates, 2002), 20.
34. Michel Foucault, *Power/Knowledge* (Brighton: Harvester Wheatsheaf, 1980), 11.

Through *interactions* in the social structure, students begin to *internalize* the social expectations, behaviours and values of the profession and are *socialized* into the institutional culture and church tradition. At this stage, students are very sensitive to how others perceive them and whether they are doing things right. They are likely to want to know the rules of appropriate action and appropriate behaviour: they will look to authority figures for direction and for reassurance that they are doing well and fitting in. An important consequence of daily interaction with others is their *social construction of reality*.

Individual Level

Individual identity formation happens at a personality level "which involves the intra-psychic domain of human functioning traditionally studied by developmental psychologists and psychoanalysts, and is referred to as the psyche, the self, cognitive structure, etc. depending on the school of thought."[35]

During interactions students attempt to manage others' impressions of them and the identity they seek to portray. This performative aspect of self may become unconscious with continual role rehearsal and may be influenced by the institutional culture. The students need to achieve a social self-concept and sense of self-esteem that drives the process. The person's identity can be classified at three levels:[36]

- *Social identity* refers to the person's position in the culture and the pressure to fit into the accepted cultural roles. Here personal style allows for individuality.
- *Personal identity* refers to the fit between a person's social identity as "theological student" and his or her unique life history.
- *Ego identity* is a fundamentally subjective sense of continuity that is characteristic with personality. It is affected by intra-psychic factors and biological dispositions.

Students also know how to "behave" and "survive" in the environment. This is especially so in the case of needing to be recommended for ordination when students will not jeopardize their chances. Students can become identity

---

35. Cote and Levine, *Identity, Formation*, 65.
36. Cote and Levine, 73–75.

diffused, dependent on concrete day-to-day validation and direction from others rather than maintaining an internal frame of reference,[37] with the tendency to hide parts of their true self. This is because a person's self-concept and social identity become matters for survival.

From the above summary, through corporate and individual processes the social structure is maintained or altered, interactions can become normalized (even becoming discrimination) or disrupted, and the individual's personality is continued or change is promoted. The social structure is reproduced when the status quo is maintained, institutional culture is transmitted and the social control mechanisms are applied.[38] The student gradually becomes more proficient with the tasks, vocabulary and organizing principles of the professional community. In this way, competence becomes more aligned with the role of pastor in a process of identity formation.

Implications for Theological Education

Identity develops in interactional relationships over time and is more influenced by the hidden curriculum than by formal teaching experiences. The social structure of the seminary culture is where students are being formed, positively or negatively. Within seminaries there are embodied patterns of behaviour, established over time as "the way things are done," within hierarchical settings. Some groups in organizations are more powerful than others – leadership, management, staff and the dominant culture, which are able to manipulate the cultural signals and message which the institution projects both internally and externally. Within seminary culture students are being educated and formed inside the ethos and values of the broader church denomination, which often is patriarchal and hierarchical with its authoritarianism.[39] For example, because of sexist ecclesial attitudes and practices, women often experience the abuse of patriarchal privilege. The problem with this is that there is a failure to see

---

37. Cote and Levine, 100.

38. Anthony Giddens, *The Constitution of Society: Outline of the Theory of Structuration* (Cambridge: Polity, 1964).

39. Marilyn Naidoo, "An Ethnographic Study on Managing Diversity in Two Protestant Theological Colleges," *HTS Theological Studies* 72, no. 1 (2016): 1–7.

how all sorts of language and behaviour reinforce what continues to be an uneven playing field.

It is important to note that the relationship between the faculty, staff and students communicates potent messages about the nature of leadership and community. As Shaw states, "If unresolved interpersonal conflicts exist within the school, students will not take seriously lessons that urge the centrality of reconciliation and peacemaking in the leadership of Christian faith communities."[40] Students rapidly come to understand power relationships within the theological community and subconsciously take that model into their work.

It should be noted that social interaction is fundamental to the process of identity development. Theological institutions should be alert to the socially constructed nature of identity[41] as it is impossible to know one's self outside the cultural and gender socialization that informs one's life. Since identity is socially constructed it can be socially deconstructed and reconstructed or changed to enable positive interactions for identity formation. We need to confront systems of oppression, such as institutional racism and sexism embedded in our institutions. We may have to recognize "that institutional policies may be culturally bound and may reflect the dominant culture" and may inadvertently privilege some groups.[42] According to Christerson and others, the "transformation of identities [is] more likely to occur when people from society's dominant social group are aware of their privileged position and willing to compromise."[43] Awareness of the messaging and engaging in difficult discussions will help towards inclusion.

---

40. Perry Shaw, *Transforming Theological Education* (Carlisle: Langham Global Library, 2014), 87.

41. Elizabeth J. Tisdell and Derise E. Tolliver, "Claiming a Sacred Face: The Role of Spirituality and Cultural Identity in Transformative Adult Higher Education," *Journal of Transformative Education* 1, no. 4 (2003): 368–392.

42. Allison N. Ash and Laurie A Schreiner, "Pathways to Success for Students of Colour in Christian Colleges: The Role of Institutional Integrity and Sense of Community," *Christian Higher Education* 15, no. 1–2 (2016): 41.

43. Brad Christerson, Korie L. Edwards and Michael O. Emerson, *Against All Odds: The Struggle for Racial Integration in Religious Organizations* (New York: New York University Press, 2005), 161.

In the classroom it would also involve engaging students where they are and unpacking their social location, which helps to bring issues of identity to the forefront, so that students can engage with intersections between their religious beliefs, theological constructions and the social realities. Students are human beings who bring with them their own narratives and life stories, including multiple strengths and vulnerabilities. It helps students see how their own social locations predispose them to interpret behaviour. And as students reflect further, distinct value sets, views of the "other" and understandings of the world begin to surface. The idea is that if students can begin to articulate and affirm their own diverse cultural identities – their essentially multifaceted selves – then they will be in a better position to engage "others" who are different from them as well. If everyone is "intercultural" in some way or other, then it becomes harder to reduce "others" to uncritical stereotypes. Changing how one sees another requires an ongoing conscious effort, and it can only begin when a student starts to question him- or herself in relation to his or her projections of difference. This will, of course, involve disruption of meaning, knowledge and comfort zones, but the freedom to make known *who* I am, to construct and make known my individual life story as identity, affords me the right to be somebody. Equal dignity implies that the unique identity of every individual be recognized. This process of conscientization[44] allows for students to reflect on social location and identity construction, from confrontation of the system to self-awareness to re-articulation.[45] For example, as graduates make the transition to ministry, they would do well to consider what life-cycle issues face them. A person entering ministry at mid-life stage would reflect differently on academic studies and supervision would also impact ministry differently. It is here that students can reflect on their social identity and how areas of psychological vulnerability shape that transition.

Finally, since the formation of identity is produced through both individual cognition *and* sociocultural processes which construct knowledge, theological educators need to maximize the opportunities that exist in the various

---

44. Paulo Freire, *Pedagogy of the Oppressed* (New York: Continuum, 1970).

45. Jack A. Hill, "Fighting the Elephant in the Room: Ethical Reflections on White Privilege and Other Systems of Advantage in the Teaching of Religion," *Teaching Theology & Religion* 12, no. 1 (2009): 3–23.

relational settings. Since role models and mentors play an important part by demonstrating appropriate behaviour, educators should provide appropriate feedback, reflective exercises and opportunities to experiment. Educators should provide the pedagogical space to understand developing identities. Self-awareness workshops are helpful. Educators also need to attend to discriminatory structures within the institution and to support intrapersonal work where the student attempts to make conceptual changes in his or her beliefs and actions.

Conclusion

Education in its broadest sense is about the transformation of the self into new ways of thinking and relating. The PSSP model of identity development highlights the importance of the sociocultural context as an environment for formation *and* the inner workings processes on the individual. This awareness of how seminary institutional culture is shaping students corporately and individually is an attempt to see our responsibility to form students more holistically. In this way, we begin to close the secular-sacred gap, by involving the developing human person in holistic formation. Once we open the door to the way of becoming a person, we open the door to a deeper and more complex discussion involving the agency of the Holy Spirit, the role of the human will, the place of the Word, the nature of the heart and the necessity of relationships with others. As Willard reminds us, "the inner dimensions of the human being result in transformation of the whole person, including the body in its social context."[46] Theological educators should also encourage the development of lifelong formative practices that help nurture a leader's sense of vocation, which makes for a richer vision of Christian leadership.

Questions for Personal Reflection and Group Discussion

1. Discuss the degree to which identity formation for ministry is present as a particular emphasis in the curriculum and culture of your theological institution.

---

46. Dallas Willard, *The Spirit of Discipline: Understanding How God Changes Lives* (New York: Harper, 1988).

2. If present (perhaps by another name), how is identity formation understood to relate to other aspects of ministerial formation, such as spiritual formation?

3. Evaluate ways in which a greater emphasis on identity formation would contribute to the self-understanding of students and graduates, with regards to their diverse callings and ministerial vocations, and their roles and responsibilities within society as Christians and Christian leaders. Do you see any problems with emphasizing identity formation in your context?

4. Based upon the observation of your own cultural context or particular church context, discuss common misconceptions of Christian leadership and discipleship that serve to deepen the sacred-secular divide. What underlying assumptions contribute to this dualistic vision of Christian life and ministry?

5. Pray for Christian leaders of different denominations in your local churches, city and country.

6. Reflect on ways in which a balanced and holistic understanding of Christian leadership and discipleship might be extended and reinforced within the institutional culture and training programs of local churches through the ministry and influence of the teachers, students and graduates of your institution.

7. Within the framework provided by the PSSP model, share examples of collective and individual self-identity that you consider to be essential aspects of a biblical understanding of Christian vocation, ministry and leadership. Discuss the implications of the examples mentioned for the ways in which Christians relate to society, as they live and minister beyond the four walls of the church.

8. Pray for wisdom to apply any new insights into your own ministry and teaching and into the institutional life of your seminary.

References

Ash, Allison N., and Laurie A. Schreiner. "Pathways to Success for Students of Colour in Christian Colleges: The Role of Institutional Integrity and Sense of Community." *Christian Higher Education* 15, no. 1–2 (2016): 38–61.

Cetuk, Virginia S. *What to Expect in Seminary: Theological Education as Spiritual Formation*. Nashville: Abingdon, 1998.

Christerson, Brad, Korie L. Edwards and Michael O. Emerson. *Against All Odds: The Struggle for Racial Integration in Religious Organizations*. New York: New York University Press, 2005.

Coe, John. "Resisting the Temptation of Moral Formation: Opening to Spiritual Formation in the Cross and Spirit." *Journal of Spiritual Formation and Soul Care* 1, no. 1 (2008): 54–78.

Cote, James E., and Charles G. Levine. *Identity, Formation, Agency and Culture*. Mahwah, NJ: Lawrence Erlbaum Associates, 2002.

Erickson, Erik H. *Identity: Youth and Crisis*. New York: Norton, 1968.

Estep, James R., and Jonathan H. Kim. *Christian Formation: Integrating Theology and Human Development*. Nashville: B&H, 2010.

Foster, Charles, Lisa Dahill, Larry Golemon and Barbara Tolentino. *Educating Clergy: Teaching Practices and Pastoral Imaginations*. San Francisco: Jossey-Bass, 2006.

Foucault, Michel. *Power/Knowledge*. Brighton: Harvester Wheatsheaf, 1980.

Freire, Paulo. *Pedagogy of the Oppressed*. New York: Continuum, 1970.

Giddens, Anthony. *The Constitution of Society: Outline of the Theory of Structuration*. Cambridge: Polity, 1964.

Grenz, Stanley J. *Theology for the Community of God*. Grand Rapids, MI: Eerdmans, 1994.

Heitink, Gerben. *Practical Theology: History, Theory, Action Domains – Manual for Practical Theology*. Grand Rapids, MI: Eerdmans, 1993.

Hill, Jack A. "Fighting the Elephant in the Room: Ethical Reflections on White Privilege and Other Systems of Advantage in the Teaching of Religion." *Teaching Theology & Religion* 12, no. 1 (2009): 3–23.

House, James S. "The Three Faces of Social Psychology." *Sociometry* 40, no. 2 (1977): 161–177.

Hughes, Richard T. *The Vocation of a Christian Scholar: How Christian Faith Can Sustain the Life of the Mind*. Grand Rapids, MI: Eerdmans, 2005.

Jones, Gregory, and Kevin Armstrong. *Resurrecting Excellence: Shaping Faithful Christian Ministry*. Grand Rapids, MI: Eerdmans, 2006.

Lawler, Steph. *Identity: Sociological Perspectives*. Cambridge: Polity, 2008.

Liefeld, Walter, and Linda Cannell. "Spiritual Formation and Theological Education." In *Alive to God: Studies in Spirituality*, edited by J. I. Packer and Loren Wilkinson, 239–252. Downers Grove, IL: InterVarsity Press, 1992.

Marsden, George M. *Evangelicalism and Modern America*. Grand Rapids, MI: Eerdmans, 1984.

Marshall, Joretta. "Formative Practices: Intent, Structure, and Content." *Reflective Practice: Formation and Supervision in Ministry* 29 (2009): 56–72.

Naidoo, Marilyn. "An Empirical Study on Spiritual Formation at Theological Training Institutions in South Africa." *Religion and Theology* 18, no. 4 (2011): 118–146.

———. "An Ethnographic Study on Managing Diversity in Two Protestant Theological Colleges." *HTS Theological Studies* 72, no. 1 (2016): 1–7.

———. "Ministerial Formation and Practical Theology." *International Journal of Practical Theology* 19, no. 1 (2015): 1–25.

Noll, Mark A. *Between Faith and Criticism*. Vancouver: Regent College Pub., 2004.

Palmer, Parker. *The Courage to Teach: Exploring the Inner Landscape of a Teacher's Life*. San Francisco: Jossey-Bass, 2007.

Parker, David. "Evangelical Spirituality Reviewed." *The Evangelical Quarterly* 63, no. 2 (1991): 123–148.

Pearcey, Nancy R. *Total Truth: Liberating Christianity from Its Cultural Captivity*. Wheaton, IL: Crossway, 2004.

Peskett, Howard, and Vinoth Ramachandra. *The Message of Mission*. Bangalore: SAIACS Press, 2003.

Porter, Steve L. "Sanctification in a New Key: Relieving Evangelical Anxieties over Spiritual Formation." *Journal of Spiritual Formation and Soul Care* 1, no. 2 (2008): 129–148.

Shaw, Perry. *Transforming Theological Education*. Carlisle: Langham Global Library, 2014.

Smith, James K. A. *Desiring the Kingdom: Worship Worldview and Cultural Formation*. Grand Rapids, MI: Baker Academic, 2009.

Starke, Rodney, and Roger Finke. *Acts of Faith: Explaining the Human Side of Religion*. Berkeley, CA: University of California Press, 2000.

Stott, John. *The Contemporary Christian*. Downers Grove, IL: InterVarsity Press, 1992.

Tisdell, Elizabeth J., and Derise E. Tolliver. "Claiming a Sacred Face: The Role of Spirituality and Cultural Identity in Transformative Adult Higher Education." *Journal of Transformative Education* 1, no. 4 (2003): 368–392.

Willard, Dallas. *The Spirit of Discipline: Understanding How God Changes Lives*. New York: Harper, 1988.

Section 3

A Call to the Church

In the world of ICETE there is frequent discussion, and general agreement, on the importance of theological education being both ecclesial and missional. In this section our authors draw attention to the importance of these two goals of theological education. The first focuses on the theology of work and the importance that it has in equipping the majority of Christians in their workplace. The second develops the missional importance of the workplace and the need for the church to equip people for that ministry.

In chapter 6, Tink and Reju approach the important topic of the theology of work. Drawing on numerous biblical insights they ask about *left-handed* ministers – that is, those who are not professional pastors. They focus on the people who are, after all, the majority of the church. The chapter gives a short historical survey of approaches to work, showing the Reformation re-emphasis on the value of work and the renewed interest in this area in more recent decades. Their work with Mustard Seed Foundation demonstrates some practical initiatives that encourage the church to value the theology of work.

They finish with many examples of empowerment for Christian workers in their various fields of work, as they strengthen "the left-handed ones."

Greene and Shaw begin with a poignant story of a young woman, Victoria, who as a hairdresser demonstrates practical and powerful ways of living as a Christian in her workplace. Where a divided sacred and secular experience disempowers lay Christians, a robust integration lays the foundation for far greater joy and effectiveness in workplace ministry. In harmony with the earlier authors, they call for seminaries to be alive to the importance of this equipping role. They provide many challenges and practical questions to be considered in the seminary and church context to help move beyond mere assent to the importance of this topic, to instead act upon it. They shine a light on the path to develop more missional practices by Christians within their workplaces.

6

Theology of Work and the Mustard Seed Foundation

Fletcher L. Tink and Oladotun Reju

The story is told in Judges 20:16 of seven hundred Gibeonites, described as choice men who, with their left hand, could sling a stone at a hair and not miss.

We have been intrigued by this story. Why left-handed? Why were they so accurate? Why organize a company around such a strange precondition? Were they better fighters than right-handers?

It seems that, statistically, left-handers' life-expectancy is shorter, sometimes explained by different neurological wiring, or perhaps the stress of a society tilted in favour of right-handers. One theory suggests that these men were left-handed because, as prisoners of war in earlier battles, their right arms had been chopped off, to ensure that they would never fight again. Yet surprisingly they reskilled themselves for battle despite their deficiency. And they were the best!

For eleven years, the Mustard Seed Foundation has been presenting seminars around the world to again focus the church on the importance of training so-called laypeople to see themselves as trained left-handed warriors at the forefront of mission, and doing so with a deeper understanding of the biblical commission that engages them. This chapter will argue that, despite our theological affirmation of the priesthood of all believers, we have too often resorted to relying on professional Christians – or right-handed soldiers – to engage the world with the gospel, not merely through verbal proclamation but by seeding the very structures of society with a Kingdom mindset.

This chapter reviews some theological premises, discusses the reach and range of Mustard Seed Foundation's initiatives around the world, acknowledges other similar initiatives, and offers case studies of how churches, institutions, businesses and communities are transformed by left-handed warriors.

Our Ambivalence towards the Left-Handed Types

If it be admitted that the church has often relied on right-handed professionals to be on the front lines of ministry and mission, we must ask ourselves further whether we, as professional Christians, have sliced off much of the potential of laypeople to conduct significant ministry in settings outside of the institutional church? We admit to an implicit ecclesiastical hierarchy that features missionaries, pastors, evangelists, theological professors and those receiving the official ordination imprimatur of religious organizations as the real ministers. Alongside these ministry professionals, it would appear that all others are the support cast. Indeed, it seems as if we professionals fly the world as if we were in executive or first class, while all others ride in the back of the plane in economy class.

Martin Luther spoke of the priesthood of all believers. Yet often we function in two different worlds. One group of Christians sees their context of ministry as "the church gathered," while others spend the larger part of their lives outside the formal church in the workaday world in what could be called "the church scattered." According to a common misconception, ministry in church is sacred, while all else is secular. Likewise, we often treat Sunday as sacred, while Monday through Saturday is business as normal and secularized.

Our experience has shown that this misconception has coloured the way most of our theological institutions train would-be pastors and church leaders. This, in turn, impacts how these graduates eventually lead their churches. Many believers live disconnected lives uncertain as to how, as Paul Stevens addresses it, to function as Christians on the other six days.[1]

For example, in the current reality of Nigeria and elsewhere, where churches spring up on every corner, there seems to be a lack of corresponding

---

1. R. Paul Stevens, *The Other Six Days: Vocation, Work, and Ministry in Biblical Perspective* (Grand Rapids, MI: Eerdmans, 2000).

socioeconomic and political transformation. We have been focused on preaching the quantitative gospel of salvation, with a focus on inner piety, as opposed to the qualitative gospel of the Kingdom that produces social transformation.

This reality should bring us back to one of the basic purposes of theology: to rethink our understanding of who God is and what he came to do on earth. Our theology has serious practical implications, as William Temple warns us: "If your conception of God is radically false, then the more devout you are, the worse it will be for you. You are opening yourself up to be moulded by something base; you had much better be an atheist."[2]

A biblically grounded theology of work serves as a needed corrective to the misconceptions already mentioned, and challenges our ecclesiological and missiological suppositions – indeed all aspects of theological understanding.

Perhaps we have forgotten that most heroes of the Bible were not professionally credentialled as religious leaders. We only need to call to mind Noah, the shipbuilder, Abraham, the rancher, and Joseph, the political economist and urban designer. We may also think of King David, the sheepherder and musician, Daniel, a political transplant in the midst of imperial worlds, Nehemiah, chief security officer to the king, Esther, Miss Persia and queen. New Testament examples include Luke, a medical doctor, and Priscilla and Aquila, a working corporation, perhaps led by a woman.

Most of Jesus's parables highlight contexts other than the synagogue or the temple, with many of them referring to the workplace, such as agricultural fields, judges' chambers, the marketplace, a construction site and, the most formative place of work, the home. Jesus himself spent most of his life as an understudy in a vocation sometimes poorly translated as carpenter, but better described as a profession that combined elements of both handyman and an engineer. Was God trying to tell us something in that Jesus's requisite qualification for being known as a rabbi was to first be involved in a functional occupation and creative design?

Four or more of the twelve disciples were entrepreneurs involved in the fishing industry. Two or three others, perhaps, were militants seeking to overthrow the status quo. One was a tax collector. Ironically, few would have passed theological entrance exams, and none could have produced impressive

---

2. William Temple, *Christian Faith in Life* (New York: Macmillan, 1931), 24.

ministry résumés. Yet they each had transferable skills that mirrored what they had learned in their professions despite being described as "unschooled, ordinary men" (Acts 4:13).

Paul, the consummate missionary, tells us with some satisfaction that he was self-supporting as a tentmaker, buying animal skins from the lowest of the low, the unclean tanners, and selling his handiwork to the livestock-rich Bedouins, perhaps conveying his mission at both extremes of society and to those within his professional class – Priscilla and Aquila.

The Scriptures present God as the Divine Worker, active in his creating, redeeming, sustaining and consummating roles. Jesus says of himself, "My food . . . is to do the will of him who sent me and to finish his work" (John 4:34). Jesus's own work is an extension of the Father's work and the fulfilment of the work the Father has given him to do: "My Father is always at his work to this very day, and I too am working" (John 5:17). "As long as it is day, we must do the works of him who sent me. Night is coming, when no one can work" (John 9:4).

If we are created in the image of God and then redeemed to something of our original design, we mirror to some degree his task of creating, redeeming, sustaining and consummating, though limited in time and space. There is no hint in these verses that some are called to work religiously, while others get a pass.

Biblical Perspectives for a Theology of Work

The examples mentioned above are but a part of the fruit of the seeds of a theology of work planted in the first chapters of Genesis.

In the first three chapters of Genesis, we learn that work in the garden of Eden was a noble endeavour seen as a gift from God, a grand responsibility to his creation and a primary form of worship, expressed back to God. In what many call the "creation mandate" or the "cultural mandate,"[3] humans are given multiple tasks, not to merely fill a schedule with activities and busy work, but rather to extend and embellish what God had already created.

---

3. Gregory A. Smith, "The Cultural Mandate, the Pursuit of Knowledge and the Christian Librarian," in *Christian Librarianship: Essays on the Integration of Faith and Profession* (Jefferson, NC: McFarland & Co., 2002), 29. For further discussion on the cultural mandate, see Roger S. Greenway, "The Cultural Mandate," in *Evangelical Dictionary of World Missions*, ed. A. Scott Moreau (Grand Rapids, MI: Baker, 2000), 251–252.

We find at least four components to the creation mandate of Genesis.

First, there is the command to "be fruitful" and multiply (Gen 1:28), or "be fertile" and multiply (God's Word Translation). This suggests that God loves fullness – ongoing creativity that is measured by quantity and quality in creative balance. Quantity without quality is growth gone awry, while quality without quantity is stagnation. Implicit in this are both personal development and universal enhancement.

Second, the Lord God took the man and placed him in the orchard in Eden "to care for it and to maintain it" (Gen 2:15 New English Translation). This would suggest that we are called not to own or abuse the earth, but to treat it with the love and care of a steward, serving lovingly the joyous creation of the Master. Implicit in this is the development of economic activity and structures.

Third is God's implicit passion for community. When God said that "there was still no human being to farm the fertile land" (Gen 2:5 CEB), he shows his vulnerability in desiring a partnership with human beings. Though God himself exists in inter-trinitarian community (as alluded to in Gen 1:26: "Let us make mankind in our image"), the triune God wanted to extend that community on earth as it is in heaven.

In other words, he yearns to define himself as community and to create community, and he does so by assigning an earthly couple to work alongside him as they generate their own new community. As Martin Luther King Jr suggested, God is in the business of both creating beloved communities[4] and creating humans with the potential for doing the same. Implicit in this is the development of human societies, institutions, politics and governance.

Fourth, God invited all the living creatures to parade before Adam so that names could be assigned to each genre. This is the task of taxonomies, naming and categorizing all that is around us. Until things have names, they cannot be grouped together, to be used for human good and God's glory.

This ritual of naming things is the initial task of science, from subatomic particles to quasars, from molecular structures to mammoths. Only with names can we organize and control our environment. Implicit in this is the spirit

---

4. The term "beloved community" was first coined by the early twentieth-century American philosopher Josiah Royce (1855–1916). King's understanding of the concept is given expanded treatment in Kenneth L. Smith and Ira G. Zepp Jr, *Search for the Beloved Community: The Thinking of Martin Luther King Jr* (Valley Forge: Judson Press, 1998).

of innovation and creativity that mirrors the character of God as Creator, generously reflected in all human beings.

The sad reality is that recent evangelical Christianity has so focused on the essential redemptive mandate that it has ignored the power, range and impact of the creation mandate.[5] In doing so, we have diminished the value of the great efforts of many people who are indeed honouring and living out the creation mandate.

The disobedience of the first couple brought a disastrous out-of-kilter dysfunction on the whole of creation, including work. As a consequence of the fall, work lost its transcendent purpose and became focused merely on survival. Though the ground was cursed, work itself was not. Still, as a result of sin and the curse of the ground, human effort became much more precarious, confined and counterproductive, as it seemed as if the whole of nature contrived against it. Furthermore, human corruption seeded work with a series of evils, including great economic disparities, abuses and wrongly conceived efforts. The human mandate to give creation added value now had to contend with all kinds of adverse factors that diminished value. Indeed, we contend that good work generally gives added value to those involved, to the product or service itself, and to the culture in general, whereas bad work typically diminishes value.

At times, the redemptive possibilities of work sputtered and lay dormant through human disobedience and deception. Nevertheless, much of the Bible is devoted to describing the consequences of judgment on failed human work, and God's constant effort to rehabilitate it through the various divine covenants, the founding of the nation of Israel, the sacrificial rituals, and the ceremonial and legal laws centred in the Ten Commandments. The wisdom literature, including the book of Proverbs, and the prophetic judgments also served to recall God's people to wise and faithful obedience according to his original purposes for life, work and worship.

---

5. Neal DeRoo, "Culture Regained? On the Impossibility and Meaninglessness of Culture in (Some) Calvinistic Thought," *The Kuyper Center Review*, vol. 3: *Calvinism and Culture*, ed. Gordon Graham (Grand Rapids, MI: Eerdmans, 2013), 1–22.

Historical Developments in the Theology of Work

Many early Christians were identified with the working classes – slaves, the labouring poor and those marginalized by society. The early monastic orders saw work as a complementary part of their Christian service to God.

Over time, the principle of redemption and lift brought many of these into positions of influence and power, along with the subtle pressures to segment holy work from daily work. This phenomenon has been repeated in many eras and countries throughout history.

However, Christian history notes that spirituality and material labour periodically were seen in conflict and that secular work was seen as inferior to sacred duties. The Protestant Reformation tried to recalibrate this, and later Puritan initiatives gave practical work a more positive value. The Industrial Revolution of the eighteenth and nineteenth centuries again bifurcated mental work from physical work, and spiritual exercises from menial labour.[6]

A Renewal of Interest in the Theology of Work

Over the past thirty years there has been considerable discussion resulting in numerous recent books researching the theme of a biblical understanding of work. A competent review of leading proponents of the theology of work can be found in Alistair Mackenzie's "Faith at Work: Vocation, the Theology of Work and the Pastoral Implications."[7] Additional writers are named in the footnote.[8] Many related books are narrative, written from the point of view of business people discovering their unique role in Christian service. Dennis

---

6. A detailed historical narrative can be found in Leland Ryken, *Work and Leisure in Christian Perspective* (Eugene, OR: Wipf & Stock, 2002).

7. Alistair Mackenzie, "Faith at Work: Vocation, the Theology of Work and the Pastoral Implications" (MTh thesis, University of Otago, 1997), accessed 25 August 2020, https://www.theologyofwork.org/uploads/general/Vocation-Theology-of-Work-and-Pastoral-Implications-Thesis.pdf.

8. Early proponents of a renewed understanding of work include those listed below. Dates given refer to their seminal publications in chronological order, while the dates in the bibliography reflect the most recent date of publication or revision. Larry Peabody (1974), Studs Terkel (1974), Robert Greenleaf (1977), Ray S. Anderson (1986), Robert Banks (1993), Max Stackhouse (1995), Michael Novak (1996), Os Guinness (1997), Ann Coombs (2001), William Diehl (2001), Richard Higginson (2002), Miroslav Volf (2002), Melba Maggay (2004), John Beckett (2006),

Bakke wrote *Joy at Work* (2006), which served as his impetus in the Mustard Seed Foundation initiative discussed here.

More recently, *Every Good Endeavor* (2014) by New York City pastor Timothy Keller, and two recent book series published by Hendrickson, *Theology of Work Bible Commentary* (2016) and *The Bible and Your Work Study Series* (2014–19), have added further depth to the topic.

The Roman Catholic Church has a long history of reflections on the scriptural meaning of work, including statements from two of the most recent popes. Pope John Paul II's encyclical *"Laborem Exercens"*[9] and the current Pope Francis's encyclical *"Laudato Si'"*[10] have helped raise consciousness within the Catholic Church regarding the nobility of work.

The Christian community is further indebted to the ecumenical Acton Institute located in Grand Rapids, Michigan, a think tank whose mission seeks to promote a free and virtuous society characterized by individual liberty and sustained by Judeo-Christian religious principles. Their Christian's Library Press publishes influential texts on church leadership, the vocation of work and stewardship.[11]

The Lausanne Committee for World Evangelization, founded in 1974, offered unequivocal statements on the Christian purpose of work at its Third Major Conference held in Cape Town, South Africa, in 2010. Under the heading "Truth and the Workplace," the "Cape Town Commitment" affirms:

> The Bible shows us God's truth about human work as part of God's good purpose in creation. The Bible brings the whole of

Darrell Cosden (2006), R. Paul Stevens (2006), Ben Witherington (2011), William Messenger (2013), Makoto Fujimura (2017), James Hamilton, (2017). A lengthy *Marketplace Annotated Bibliography* was published by Pete Hammond and R. Paul Stevens in 2002, expanded in 2010. Many of these authors have written multiple works on the subject of work.

9. Pope John Paul II, *"Laborem Exercens,"* accessed 25 August 2020, http://www.vatican.va/content/john-paul-ii/en/encyclicals/documents/hf_jp-ii_enc_14091981_laborem-exercens.html.

10. Pope Francis, *"Laudato Si',"* accessed 25 August 2020, http://www.vatican.va/content/francesco/en/encyclicals/documents/papa-francesco_20150524_enciclica-laudato-si.html. For a critique of these encyclicals, see Jonathan Malesic, "Why We Need a New Theology of Work," *America: The Jesuit Review*, 12 September 2016, accessed 25 August 2020, https://www.americamagazine.org/politics-society/2016/09/01/why-we-need-new-theology-work.

11. More information on Acton Institute can be found at www.acton.org. Two of their more recent books are Lester DeKoster's *Work: The Meaning of Your Life* and Gene Edward Veith's *Working for Our Neighbor: A Lutheran Primer on Vocation, Economics and Ordinary Life.*

our working lives within the sphere of ministry, as we serve God in different callings. By contrast, the falsehood of a "sacred-secular divide" has permeated the Church's thinking and action. This divide tells us that religious activity belongs to God, whereas other activity does not. Most Christians spend most of their time in work which they may think has little spiritual value (so-called secular work). But God is Lord of *all* of life. "Whatever you do, work at it with all your heart, as working for the Lord, not for men," said Paul, to slaves in the pagan workplace.[12]

This is further emphasized by this call to action: "We encourage all believers to accept and affirm their own daily ministry and mission as being wherever God has called them to work. We challenge pastors and church leaders to support people in such ministry – in the community and in the workplace – "to equip the saints for works of service [ministry]" – in every part of their lives."[13]

Very prominent in seminars at the conference, and in an entire track of online literature, is its rubric of "Business as Mission," focusing largely on the practical side of work as mission with attention to Christian influence as expressed in art, politics, business, media and public discourse. In addition to the publications mentioned, many helpful web pages are now proliferating on the theme.[14]

Recent Contributions to the Development of Reflection and Practice around the Theology of Work

Numerous Christian educational institutions have attempted in different ways to integrate theology of work courses into their curricula. Some schools, such as Gordon College, Seattle Pacific University, Laidlaw College and Regent University, offer courses related to theology of work. Other schools, such as

---

12. Lausanne Movement, "The Cape Town Commitment: A Confession of Faith and a Call to Action" (2011), IIA.3, accessed 25 August 2020, https://www.lausanne.org/content/ctcommitment.

13. Lausanne Movement, "Cape Town Commitment," IIA.3(b).

14. See Lausanne Movement, "Business as Mission," www.lausanne.org/networks/issues/business-as-mission; Bam Global: Business as Mission, www.bamglobal.org; Business as Mission, www.businessasmission.com; and Theology of Work Project, www.theologyofwork.org.

Gordon-Conwell Seminary, Luther Seminary and Concordia College, offer an entire track or specialization, while schools such as Seattle Pacific University and Biola University have developed business schools and degrees with a focus on marketplace ministries. Other schools avail themselves of special theology of work seminars designed for the Christian community at large.

The authors of this article have been deeply involved in the initiative of Bakke Graduate University (BGU) in this area of theology of work. One of the important ways in which BGU has advanced action and reflection around this vital subject is through the creation of educational tracks and degrees that focus on the theme. Other graduate institutions are now doing the same.

The Mustard Seed Foundation, a parallel initiative closely related to BGU, has advanced the initiative through seminars and classes taught throughout the world. The curriculum is based on Paul Steven's writings on the theology of work and the practical and transformational works of Dennis Bakke's experience in business which apply Christian principles of service from the bottom up, giving decision-making and teamwork a whole new shared sense of participation and fun on the job.

Alistair Mackenzie has done a brief overview of the various ways by which these schools seek to integrate theology of work. His conclusions address the challenge associated with declining enrolment and demand versus the cost of maintaining or expanding these offerings.[15] In response to this challenge, Mustard Seed Foundation's International Theology of Work Grant Program has subsidized courses at many academic institutions around the world which otherwise would not be able to fund them.[16]

Promoting Theology of Work through Strategic Funding and Equipping Initiatives

From 2007 to 2018, the Mustard Seed Foundation awarded 414 grants to provide theology of work courses internationally in a wide range of languages.

---

15. Alistair Mackenzie, "Seminaries Teaching Theology of Work," accessed 25 August 2020, https://www.theologyofwork.org/resources/seminaries-teaching-theology-of-work.

16. TOW International Theology of Work Grant Program, https://www.theologyofworkgrant.com/.

These grants engaged almost fifty-five thousand participants in seventy-eight different countries. Over the course of eleven years, almost $3 million dollars was awarded to help with tuition costs, seminar expenses and transportation costs of participants and facilitators. Often, the institutions sought grants from Mustard Seed to offer two sequential courses over a two-year period: the basic theology of work course (sometimes called "Joy at Work") and "Ethics and Responsible Business Practice."

In most presentations, the organizers insist on the participation of entrepreneurs, or make scheduled visits to the work venues of business people. Often business people are involved in our seminars (for instance, in Bangladesh, our entire group of fifty Muslim business leaders and students were affiliated with the local Rotary Club). In Alexandria, Egypt, ninety-eight Muslim leaders (out of 129 present) were bussed to the seminar.

Sometimes on our site visits, we encounter Christian business people who have not thought through their influence in their context. This gives us the opportunity to lovingly and carefully suggest to them a different approach. Others are amazingly attuned to their commission to be salt and light in their context.

The presentations are dynamic and varied, making use of Power Point presentations, spontaneous drama, singing, group sessions, testimonials, symbolic artefacts, demonstrations, video clips, readings and learning reports. The sessions vary from two-day workshops to full forty-five hours of accredited coursework.

Impact of Theology of Work Seminars on Participants and Facilitators

Space permits only a few representative examples of the many ways in which Mustard Seed Foundation's theology of work seminars impact both facilitators and participants from a variety of backgrounds.

Regarding his experience as facilitator, Fletcher Tink relates:

> I've had the privilege of teaching in twenty-four nations, in such places as eleven cities in Pakistan, six years in Nepal, in Zimbabwe, Senegal, Ethiopia, Egypt, a variety of sites in India, Bangladesh,

Cuba, Bolivia, China, Thailand, Lebanon, and for numerous institutions in the Philippines where I reside. I've had the privilege of teaching large numbers of Catholics in Pakistan, Hindus in Nepal, and Muslims in Egypt, Pakistan and Bangladesh, and was even invited to teach multiple times in Lumbini, Nepal, at the birthplace of the Buddha in a Buddhist convent.

I have found that Christians are hungry for a new sense of mission that engages all in the redemptive purposes of God.

Tink notes that the theology of work seminars have proven to be great opportunities for Christian witness and engagement with participants of other religions.

Muslims are surprised that I take God seriously as a full seven-day commitment, and have been very open to this teaching. Hindus critique the corruption in their own nations and seek ways of changing their societies through a new ethical paradigm. Buddhists appreciate the asceticism and care implicit in responsible stewardship of the created world.

I make it clear that I am not evangelizing. I am merely sowing seeds that present an alternative way of looking at the universe, filled with meaning and transcendence. At their Iftar parties, the Muslim imams are impressed that I am willing to fast with them through their days of Ramadan, though with Christian motivations.

Oladotun Reju offers insight into his experiences as a facilitator of theology of work (TOW) training in Africa and the Caribbean:

I have had the privilege of teaching theology of work in ten African countries and three islands in the Caribbean. The major part of my TOW teaching has been with two organizations in Nigeria: the Nigerian Baptist Convention, a major denomination in Nigeria of more than six million members, and the Nigeria Fellowship of Evangelical Students with student membership in all tertiary institutions in Nigeria. I have also been privileged to serve the Nigerian Baptist Theological Seminary [NBTS], Ogbomosho,

Nigeria, for five years, training seminary faculty and staff. NBTS has now included theology of work as a core course in their bachelor's degree programme.

My doctoral dissertation was inspired by theology of work and serves as the design for the Centre for Transformational Leadership, a ministry of the church I pastor in Jos, Nigeria. The centre has theology of work as its primary focus and flagship course, training emerging leaders and granting certificates and diplomas in three basic areas: business, arts and political governance.[17]

Theology of Work Case Studies

The strategic investment, both financial and educational, in teaching men and women to put principles of theology of work into practice in their daily lives and contexts has borne much fruit. Here are some examples of theology of work in action:

- A department store owner in Chennai, India, has a counselling room for his workers and clients, and gives them CDs of the Christian music he has produced.
- A molasses transport company in Armenia, Colombia, had a chapel built next to their garage where the owner conducts services and prayer groups for his employees.
- A Chinese Filipino family which owns thirteen fried chicken franchises in Zamboanga, Mindanao, quit selling liquor and now devotes a considerable portion of its profits to the financial needs of the community. This family introduced us to their major competitor who owns sixteen franchise restaurants. When we expressed surprise at their close friendship, they informed me that they do not compete, but instead share their dreams, their business strategies and Christian purposes.

---

17. Details of the centre are published on the International Theology of Work Grant website, www.theologyofworkgrant.com.

- A gynaecologist who ran a hospital in India was wrongly accused by a competitor of stealing women's body parts for sale in the USA. For several months, clients refused to come, believing the malicious rumours. Then in prayer she came up with a plan to give free tests to show that women's uteruses were intact. Slowly, clients returned, and within a period of time her business doubled, as her integrity was proven.

- A Tamil Nadu congressman, while sharing his story with us, was interrupted by his Muslim fellow congressman, and later by his Hindu peer. As we quizzed them, the two non-Christians testified that this man was their beloved brother who prays with them when they have troubles.

- Another Indian politician showed us some of the two thousand Bibles he gives to his constituents each year.

- A pastor in the Philippines has left his church to organize Motocross races on Sunday mornings. Before the motorbike races, he conducts a service to the thousands gathered, and then during the week he disciples the racers and the motorcycle business people he has networked.

There are hundreds of stories like this that could be shared. Others cannot be shared here because of their sensitive nature, but we invite you to imagine and pray for Christians around the world who are putting their theology of work training into practice to address structural issues in their own contexts, often at great personal risk.

To these testimonies of the impact that theology of work training has had in countries and local communities around the world, Oladotun Reju adds his own of the way that the creation mandate and theology of work perspectives have shaped the ministry of his local church to become salt and light in his own community:

> The most profound experience of TOW has been its impact on my congregation. The Kingdom Citizens Pavilion community in Jos, Nigeria, can be described using Larry Peabody's phrase as "a TOW-woven ministry." We operate an elementary and a high

school where the TOW concept has been inculcated into every subject in the school.

The critical question every teacher needs to ask him- or herself is "What can I include in my teaching that will foster the call of God upon my pupils and students?" My joy knew no bounds the day I read the assignment of a 12-year-old student on a subject that has to do with forest preservation and identified the guard working to preserve the forest as a co-redeemer working with God to restore shalom to God's creation. Our students now choose a career path as their pursuit of the call of God upon their lives.

Our local church community is described as a church of one hundred and fifty parishes, where we gather on Sundays. All the parishes fit into a little hall and, as we scatter from Monday through Saturday, we serve God's purposes to our city in various centres and ways. Our Bible study groups are divided along vocational and professional lines where each group studies the Bible through the prism of the callings. As of 2019, we have professional discipleship groups of health workers, artists, business people, along with those interested in public service and politics.

Every member of our church who just graduated from school or any other vocational training is taken through a specialized TOW course to be ordained into ministry. We do not feature traditional ordination evidenced by titles in our church. Instead we practise Luther's universal priesthood of the believer in our church life.

Next Steps for Mustard Seed's Theology of Work Program

As the Mustard Seed Foundation looks to the future, the leadership seeks to build on what has been learned and accomplished in the past years and to define priorities for strategic partnerships, funding and equipping opportunities. In this regard, Lowell Bakke, Mustard Seed's chief architect of theology of work, explains: "One of the goals will be to invest in a team of schools and organizations from around the world who will be able to take the TOW message to more and more places well beyond the shelf life of the Foundation. In this five-year period, we desire to work with as many ICETE schools as possible."

Through this new phase of cooperation, Mustard Seed aims

> to expose and train professors in the area of faith and work through the Theology of Work Grant Program. This will begin with a nine-week online (Zoom Room) TOW course delivered by Bakke Graduate University. This course will be specifically for ICETE schools. Part of the online course will require that the professors develop a contextualized Theology of Work grant course specifically designed for their school which could be co-taught with one of the certified International TOW faculty, assisted by a TOW grant. A faculty member from the grant program will be assigned as a mentor throughout the course development and grant development and teaching phase at the grantee school. Our plan is to work with three regions through a period of three years.[18]

Conclusion

The hope of Mustard Seed Foundation is to transfer theology of work initiatives from the core base of faculty to a much more inclusive range of professors who would be more regionally based, institutionally committed and contextually insightful. Since the ICETE conference in Panama, the worldwide COVID-19 pandemic has offered new opportunities to express theology of work without the barriers of time and space. The curriculum is being developed on multiple fronts and in contextualized ways through the Internet, and may ultimately reach a far greater audience of Christians who have an expanded understanding of their role in the workplace. It is also hoped that the voice of women will resonate with greater precision and expanded influence in the discussions around the world.

---

18. Updated information can be found at www.theologyofworkgrant.com.

Our prayer is that the left-handed warriors will rise up around the world and put their adapted skills, insights and practice to work in order to become a more integral part of the whole message of God to the whole world.

Questions for Personal Reflection and Group Discussion

1. The authors describe the preference shown by some churches and theological institutions for right-handed ministry professionals over left-handed lay ministers. They argue that this bias relegates Monday to Saturday marketplace ministry to a plane of lesser importance than Sunday ministry within the church. Does this characterization ring true in your own context? If so, how is this preference communicated (explicitly or implicitly) by theological institutions and the church?

2. Evaluate the degree to which the renewal of interest in the theology of work in recent decades has been felt within your own theological institution and the churches of your context. Share examples that illustrate the impact (or lack of impact) of a biblical understanding of work.

3. As you reflect on the theology of work case studies shared by the authors, what examples and testimonies can you add from your own context of left-handed lay Christians ministering faithfully and missionally within the context of their professional or vocational occupations?

4. In response to the authors' invitation, pause "to imagine and pray for Christians around the world who are putting their theology of work training into practice to address structural issues in their own contexts, often at great personal risk."

5. To what degree are these topics integral in your institution's teaching and program: the creation mandate; the priesthood of all believers; other biblical foundations of a theology of work? Discuss strategies that the seminaries and churches in your context could develop to help both ministry professionals and lay Christians to faithfully live out the implications of this teaching in their particular vocations and day-to-day work. Might this be a new direction/ opportunity for your seminary? Think of several Christian friends not in full-time ministry. Pray for them by name and for their ministries.

References

Anderson, Ray S. *Minding God's Business*. Eugene, OR: Wipf & Stock, 2008.

Bakke, Dennis W. *Joy at Work: A Revolutionary Approach to Fun on the Job*. Seattle: PVG, 2005.

Banks, Robert. *God the Worker: Journey into the Mind, Heart and Imagination of God*. Eugene, OR: Wipf & Stock, 2008.

Beckett, John, and Ken Blanchard. *Mastering Monday: A Guide to Integrating Faith and Work*. Downers Grove, IL: InterVarsity Press, 2009.

Benefiel, Margaret. *Soul at Work: Spiritual Leadership in Organizations*. New York: Seabury, 2005.

Coombs, Ann. *Living Workplace: Soul, Spirit and Success in the 21st Century*. Toronto: HarperCollins Canada, 2001.

Cosden, Darrell. *A Theology of Work: Work and the New Creation*. Eugene, OR: Wipf & Stock, 2006.

DeKoster, Lester. *Work: The Meaning of Your Life*. Grand Rapids, MI: Christian's Library Press, 2015.

DeRoo, Neal. "Culture Regained? On the Impossibility and Meaninglessness of Culture in (Some) Calvinistic Thought." *The Kuyper Center Review*. Vol. 3: *Calvinism and Culture*, edited by Gordon Graham, 1–22. Grand Rapids, MI: Eerdmans, 2013.

Diehl, William E. *The Monday Connection: On Being an Authentic Christian in a Weekday World*. Eugene, OR: Wipf & Stock, 2012.

Fujimura, Makoto, and Mark Labberton. *Reconnecting with Beauty for Our Common Life*. Downers Grove, IL: InterVarsity Press, 2017.

Greenleaf, Robert K. *Servant Leadership: A Journey into the Nature of Legitimate Power and Greatness*. 25th anniversary edition. Edited by Larry Spears. New York: Paulist Press, 2002.

Greenway, Roger S. "The Cultural Mandate." In *Evangelical Dictionary of World Missions*, edited by A. Scott Moreau, 251–252. Grand Rapids, MI: Baker, 2000.

Guinness, Os. *The Call: Finding and Fulfilling God's Purpose for Your Life*. Anniversary edition. Nashville: Thomas Nelson, 2008.

Hamilton, Jr., James M. *Work and Our Labor in the Lord*. Wheaton, IL: Crossway, 2017.

Hammond, Pete, R. Paul Stevens and Todd Svanoe. *The Marketplace Annotated Bibliography: A Christian Guide to Books on Work, Business and Vocation*. Downers Grove, IL: IVP Academic, 2010.

Higginson, Richard, et al. *Questions of Business Life: Exploring Workplace Issues from a Christian Perspective*. Milton Keynes: Authentic, 2002.

Keller, Tim. *Every Good Endeavor: Connecting Your Work to God's Work*. New York: Penguin Random House, 2014.

Lausanne Movement. "The Cape Town Commitment: A Confession of Faith and a Call to Action." 2011. Accessed 25 August 2020. https://www.lausanne.org/content/ctcommitment.

Mackenzie, Alistair. "Faith at Work: Vocation, the Theology of Work and the Pastoral Implication." MTh thesis, University of Otago, 1997. Accessed 25 August 2020. https://www.theologyofwork.org/uploads/general/Vocation-Theology-of-Work-and-Pastoral-Implications-Thesis.pdf.

———. "Seminaries Teaching Theology of Work." Accessed 25 August 2020. https://www.theologyofwork.org/resources/seminaries-teaching-theology-of-work.

Maggay, Melba Padilla. *Transforming Society*. Eugene, OR: Wipf & Stock, 2010.

Malesic, Jonathan. "Why We Need a New Theology of Work." *America: The Jesuit Review*, 12 September 2016. Accessed 25 August 2020. https://www.americamagazine.org/politics-society/2016/09/01/why-we-need-new-theology-work.

Messenger, William. *Calling: A Biblical Perspective*. Theology of Work Topics 1. Cambridge: Theology of Work Project, 2013. Kindle.

Messenger, William, ed. *The Bible and Your Work Study Series*. Peabody: Hendrickson Publishing, 2014–19.

———. *Theology of Work Bible Commentary*. Peabody, MA: Hendrickson, 2015–.

Novak, Michael, and Jana Novak. *Business as a Calling: Work and the Examined Life*. New York: Free Press, 2013.

Peabody, Larry. *Curing Sunday Spectatoritis: From Passivity to Participation in Church*. Portland, OR: Urban Loft Publishers, 2016.

———. *Serving Christ in the Workplace*. Fort Washington: CLC Ministries, 2004.

Pope Francis. "*Laudato Si'*." Accessed 25 August 2020. http://www.vatican.va/content/francesco/en/encyclicals/documents/papa-francesco_20150524_enciclica-laudato-si.html.

Pope John Paul II. "*Laborem Exercens*." Accessed 25 August 2020. http://www.vatican.va/content/john-paul-ii/en/encyclicals/documents/hf_jp-ii_enc_14091981_laborem-exercens.html.

Ryken, Leland. *Work and Leisure in Christian Perspective*. Eugene, OR: Wipf & Stock, 2002.

Smith, Gregory A. *Christian Librarianship: Essays on the Integration of Faith and Profession*. Jefferson, NC: McFarland & Co., 2002.

Smith, Kenneth L., and Ira G. Zepp Jr. *Search for the Beloved Community: The Thinking of Martin Luther King Jr.* Valley Forge: Judson Press, 1998.

Stackhouse, Max Lynn, Peter L. Berger, M. Douglas Meeks and Dennis McCann. *Christian Social Ethics in a Global Era*. Nashville: Abingdon, 1995.

Stevens, R. Paul. *The Other Six Days: Vocation, Work and Ministry in Biblical Perspective*. Grand Rapids, MI: Eerdmans, 2000.

Temple, William. *Christian Faith in Life*. New York: Macmillan, 1931.

Terkel, Studs. *Working: People Talk about What They Do All Day and How They Feel about What They Do*. New York: MJF Books, 2004.

Veith, Gene Edward. *Working for Our Neighbor: A Lutheran Primer on Vocation, Economics and Ordinary Life*. Grand Rapids, MI: Christian's Library Press, 2016.

Volf, Miroslav. *Work in the Spirit: Toward a Theology of Work*. Eugene, OR: Wipf & Stock, 2001.

Witherington III, Ben. *Work: A Kingdom Perspective on Labor*. Grand Rapids, MI: Eerdmans, 2011.

Some Helpful Web Pages

Bam Global: Business as Mission – www.bamglobal.org

Business as Mission – www.businessasmission.com

Lausanne Movement – "Business as Mission" www.lausanne.org/networks/issues/business-as-mission

Shared Church – http://www.sharedchurch.com

Theology of Work Project – www.theologyofwork.org

TOW International Theology of Work Grant Program – https://www.theologyofworkgrant.com/

Worldview Matters – https://biblicalworldview.com

7

The Sacred-Secular Divide and the Mission of God

Mark Greene and Ian Shaw

Here is a true story:

Victoria is an apprentice hairdresser. She's nineteen and she's been in the job just over a month. It's a busy salon so there's always something to do and it's almost always got to be done quickly. She's enjoying it but she's been feeling the pressure. Three weeks into the job her vicar commissions her into the job. She's been more at peace since then.

I (Mark) asked her, "So what difference does being a Christian make to the way you wash someone's hair?"

Victoria responded: "I pray for them as I massage in the conditioner."

Victoria's praying is an invisible gift to her clients – soothing conditioner for the soul, not just the hair. But behind her prayers lies a whole set of beliefs:

- Victoria believes that her daily context in a hairdressing salon is important to God.
- She believes that the actual work she does is important to God, and that it can be done in a distinctive way.
- She believes that God is alive and can move in a hairdressing salon.
- She believes that God wants to bless her clients, and that she can be part of that.
- She believes in the power of prayer and in God's freedom to respond in his own way and in his own time. She doesn't need to see the

results of those prayers. Indeed, this side of heaven, for the most part, she probably won't. But it's still worth praying: God will be listening to her.

- And she's confident in the God who sends her.[1]

What kind of church community makes disciples like Victoria?

What kind of church leader produces disciples like Victoria?

What kind of seminary produces church leaders who produce disciples like Victoria?

The reality is that Victoria is rare. The vast majority of Christians, whether they be children, adolescents, young or middle-aged adults, or senior citizens, do not have a vision for daily engagement and service in the places they go to day by day: the fields, the factories, the school gates, the shops, the clubs, the offices. And the reason why they don't have such a vision is because this is not the vision that grips the global evangelical church.

Our hope is that, as a result of this book, disciples like Victoria will soon not be rare.

One of the great joys of being involved in theological education is seeing the impact of our work in the lives of our graduates and in the emphases and fruitfulness of the churches they lead. There is much to celebrate. Equally, one of the sobering responsibilities of being involved in theological education is to look at the emphases of our graduates' ministries and the culture of the churches they lead and ask ourselves if the shape of those ministries and the culture of those churches are healthy, in line with the richness of the *missio Dei* and responsive to the particular challenges of the communities they are part of.

This conference's theme – "The Secular-Sacred Divide and Theological Education" – makes an assumption that has been tested in our work at the London Institute for Contemporary Christianity (LICC), confirmed by the experience of our partners at Langham, and validated by research and testimony from across the world. Overall, the core operational culture of the global evangelical church has been shaped by dualism, by the elevation of church-based activities over Monday to Saturday engagement in God's world.

---

1. Adapted with permission from Mark Greene, *The One About . . . 8 Stories about God in Our Everyday Lives* (London: LICC, 2017).

The sacred-secular divide is evident in virtually every area of church life – from theological education to popular publishing, from the content of songs to the decoration of our buildings, from the understanding of holiness and fruitfulness in Christ to the tragic dearth of whole-life disciple-making in churches across the globe. And it is crystal clear in the dominant mission strategy of the global evangelical community.

In 2010 at the Lausanne Congress for World Evangelization in Cape Town, I (Mark) asked delegates if this was the mission strategy in the churches in their nations: "to recruit the people of God to give up some of their leisure time to support the mission initiatives of church-paid workers." Virtually everyone there agreed that it was.

Now, that strategy has borne much fruit, in all kinds of neighbourhood and community initiatives and increasing commitment to mission initiatives beyond a country's borders. However, this pastor-centred, neighbourhood-focused, gathered-church strategy essentially ignores the ministry of God's people scattered in the world in their Monday to Saturday contexts.

It's an incomplete strategy because it shrivels the potential of Christians in the world and limits the mission of God. It ignores people's daily context where they naturally meet people who don't know Jesus. The result is that 98 percent of God's people – all those not ordained to full-time church-paid ministry – are not being envisioned or equipped for discipleship and mission in the 95 percent of their time when they aren't engaged in church-based activities.

Imagine a factory where 98 percent of the people were not consciously engaged in the main work of the factory. You'd think they were crazy. We *are* crazy. But imagine if we weren't crazy.

- Imagine if the church globally had spent the last fifty years helping people to see how they could be salt, light, yeast and mustard seed at school, at university, at work.
- Imagine if we hadn't convinced our young people that farming, business, defence, banking, media, law, politics, plumbing, building and cleaning were second-class callings.
- Imagine if the thousands of God's people in those arenas had been envisioned, equipped, supported and prayed for.

After all, apart from anything else, those are the places where major decisions about our societies are made, where our nations' cultures and priorities are shaped. Can we really fulfil the Lord's command to "make disciples of all nations" (Matt 28:19) without equipping our people for the contexts they find themselves in? But inadvertently, that's generally what we have done.

The reality is that the sacred-secular divide makes lay Christians think they are second-class Christians. It diminishes the value of their daily work, it blinds them to the fruit God may be producing right where they are, it shrinks their ecclesiology to the gathered context, it prevents their recognizing how the Bible addresses all of life, and it blunts their alertness to God's action in their ordinary daily lives, cutting them off from accessing prayer, wisdom and the support of the body.

In sum, the sacred-secular divide shrinks the very scope of the gospel itself. It is an affront to the all-encompassing, all-sufficient redemptive and renewing work of Christ. It is alive and well in evangelical churches across the globe, and has been for some time. As Dorothy L. Sayers put it back in 1949:

> In nothing has the Church so lost Her hold on reality as Her failure to understand and respect the secular vocation. She has allowed work and religion to become separate departments, and is astonished to find that, as a result, the secular work of the world is turned to purely selfish and destructive ends, and that the greater part of the world's intelligent workers have become irreligious or at least uninterested in religion . . . But is it astonishing? How can anyone remain interested in a religion which seems to have no concern with nine-tenths of his life?[2]

Her point isn't just about work, it is about the gospel, and it applies today. The failure to teach work well is part of a wider failure to offer a whole-life gospel to non-believers. No wonder people (so many people in the West, at least) are not gripped by the gospel. The gospel we present rarely includes any compelling vision for the transformation of ordinary daily life. No wonder the hugely encouraging numerical growth of churches in countries such as Guatemala

---

2. D. L. Sayers, "Why Work?" In *Letters to a Diminished Church: Passionate Arguments for the Relevance of Christian Doctrine* (Nashville: Thomas Nelson, 2004).

is not followed by a decline in corruption or domestic violence, if the gospel preached has not included such concerns.

The challenge of the sacred-secular divide is aggravated by the difficulty of recognizing it in ourselves. You will not find many pastors who will say that God is not interested in people's work, studies or housework, but most churches operate that way. The power of the sacred-secular divide in pastors' lives, then, is not that they think it's true, but that it shapes their ministries anyway.

Here, for example, is a quote from a school teacher: "I spend an hour a week teaching Sunday school and they haul me up to the front of the church to pray for me." What's the second half of the quote? "The rest of the week I'm a full-time teacher and the church has never prayed for me."

Not many pastors would actually *say* that the forty hours this teacher spends teaching in a school from Monday to Friday are less important to God than the forty-five minutes he or she spends teaching Sunday school, but that is exactly what has been communicated. Where a church's praying is, there its heart is.

Similarly, the power of the sacred-secular divide in theological education is not that we ourselves believe that all of life is not important to God. We know our Bibles. No, the power of the sacred-secular divide is that most of us don't think it affects us or that we need to be part of the solution – leave that to the missiologists. But the divide is too pervasive for that. It affects our mission strategy because it has already shaped the way we read our Bibles and the way we teach doctrine.

The sacred-secular divide has affected every aspect of church life and the operational understanding of almost every doctrine. It shrinks our ecclesiology by putting more focus and value on the gathered church than on the sent church. It shrinks our pneumatology by inadvertently limiting our expectations of the action of the Spirit to particular places and particular kinds of tasks. It shrinks our soteriology by focusing on individual conversion rather than on whole-life disciple-making and the *missio Dei* . . . and so on. The sacred-secular divide has diminished our understanding of God as genuinely Lord of all, who not only created all things for his glory but who, in the aftermath of the fall, sent his Son to reconcile all things in heaven and on earth to himself, through his blood shed on the cross.

However, this is much more than a plea for a course on integral mission or workplace ministry, or for a faith and work centre. In fact, such initiatives can serve to reinforce the problem by unintentionally suggesting that this is a topic to be addressed rather than a pervasive worldview to be rooted out.

The sacred-secular divide is not like a golf ball in a fruit salad: easy to spot, easy to fish out. No, the divide is like vinegar in the juice. It affects everything.

We in the West have passed on this heretical virus to the global church. Indeed, in the two-year project on "Overcoming the Sacred-Secular Divide through Theological Education"[3] that Antony Billington and Mark Greene from LICC and Dr. Ian Shaw from the Langham Partnership conducted with theological educators from around the world, we learned that, while the sacred-secular divide manifests itself in different ways in Guatemala and Gujarat, in Singapore and Sarajevo, it remains a virulent and destructive force.

One of the practical implications of this for theological educators is the reality that most of us are part of churches that maintain the sacred-secular divide, and therefore we may never have seen what a church that successfully bridges the sacred-secular gap might look like. We may not have a picture in our minds of the kind of communities we are seeking to train our students to lead, just as we may not actually have a picture of what fruitful whole-life discipleship can look like for a hairdresser, fieldworker, university student, housewife or corporate executive.

This presents us with a particular challenge. After all, as theological educators, we rightly need to be in dialogue with the academy in our discipline, and we rightly need to be in dialogue with the denominations and churches we serve. But we cannot rely on those conversations to inform our understanding of the dynamics of the places God's people find themselves in day by day and the opportunities and challenges before them. We too need to understand not just the macro forces at work in our national cultures but also the contexts in which God's people are called to be salt and light, and to seek and pray for their shalom.

---

3. See report and recommendations for best practice in Mark Greene and Ian Shaw, eds., *Whole-Life Mission for the Whole Church: Overcoming the Sacred-Secular Divide through Theological Education* (Carlisle: Langham Global Library, 2021).

The pervasiveness of the sacred-secular divide makes our understanding of our cultural contexts even more important precisely because most of our students also come to our seminaries from sacred-secular divided churches, and on the whole go back into the same types of churches.

So the challenge to our institutions is not only to ask ourselves:

- Is my institution's culture affected by the sacred-secular divide?
- Does the sacred-secular divide affect my teaching?
- Am I affected by the sacred-secular divide?

But also to ask:

- Do we have a vision for what Monday to Saturday discipleship could look like for the people in our own churches?
- Do we know what a whole-life disciple-making church might look like?

The reason why these are important questions to ask is because such churches are extremely rare. On the whole, denominations have historically not asked seminaries to train whole-life disciple-making pastors. However, as Bishop Graham Cray, author of *Mission-Shaped Church* and former Principal of Ridley Hall, Cambridge, puts it, "Churches have to realize that the core of their calling is to be disciple-making communities, whatever else they do."[4]

To a greater degree than we often realize, our local church culture is deeply affected by the sacred-secular divide. It affects the songs we sing – rarely about Monday to Saturday life. It affects who and what's on the prayer list – rarely the Monday to Saturday mission fields of the congregation. It affects what's on the agenda of our meetings – rarely the discipling of all God's people. It affects the stories we tell in church, who we praise in public, how pastors spend their time, what they see in the Bible, what they choose to preach about, what illustrations they give.

A while back, when I (Mark) was teaching at the London School of Theology, I conducted some research on evangelical preaching.[5] We discovered

---

4. Quoted in an address given at London Institution for Contemporary Christianity in the summer of 2010. See further G. Cray, *Disciples and Citizens: A Vision for Distinctive Living* (Nottingham: Inter-Varsity Press, 2007); and G. Cray, *Who's Shaping You? 21st Century Disciples* (Harpenden: Cell UK, 2010).

5. Mark Greene, "Is Anybody Listening?," *Anvil* 14, no. 4 (1997): 283–294.

that over 50 percent of evangelicals had never heard a sermon on work and that, more significantly, a higher percentage didn't feel they had a biblical understanding of work and its role in their lives.

How could that be? After all, the Bible brims with material set at work, about work and applicable to work. From Genesis to Revelation work is a recurrent theme, in creation and fall, in the construction of the ark and of the tower, in Jacob's dealings with Laban, in Joseph's growth, in Moses's practice, in Levitical and Deuteronomic instruction and command, in the exercise of authority in Deborah and the other judges, in Kings, in Boaz's counter-cultural workplace praxis, in David's frequent pleas in the Psalms for help in his often hostile work environment, and so on through Nehemiah, Esther, Proverbs, Ecclesiastes, the Prophets, the Gospels, Philippians, Colossians, Thessalonians and Revelation.

The theme of work is all over the Bible. It is not only absolutely obvious that work is in the text, it's absolutely obviously an issue for anyone in a church who is engaged in an occupation or a profession. So why haven't evangelical preachers preached it? That is the sacred-secular divide in action. Either we don't see it, or we choose not to preach it when we do.

This is a hermeneutical issue, yes, and it's a homiletical issue and a doctrinal issue. But it's also a pastoral issue, a missional issue, a discipling issue. Somehow it is possible for graduates to leave our seminaries and not know that a core component of their ministry involves helping God's people live out their calling as royal priests in their Monday to Saturday lives. What vision, we might ask, are we passing on of the role of the Christian in the world?

This doesn't just have an impact on individuals: it has an impact on nations. In the 1950s in Germany the church asked itself: How was it that the church and the nation succumbed, for the most part, so easily to Nazism? Of course, there were a host of factors, but one of their main conclusions was this: the church did not have a robust enough doctrine of election.

Frankly, when I was told that by the researcher, I didn't understand it. And I didn't understand it because of what I thought the doctrine of election was. When I was taught the doctrine of election at college, we focused on predestination and double-predestination, on the debate between Calvin and Arminius and those who followed them – who's in, who's out, and how many. It's an important question and a very good topic to help students develop theological method – to combine exegetical, analytical, historical, philosophical and writing skills.

But that, my researcher friend pointed out, is not the heart of the doctrine of election. The heart of the doctrine is that we have been chosen as a kingdom of priests in the world with a particular role to play. If we don't understand our calling in the world we are unlikely to work to fulfil it. That is what happened to the church in Germany. And it has certainly occurred in my own nation.

This matters hugely in the local church. Who do God's people believe they are called to be? What do they think their role in the world is?

Biblical preaching and doctrinal teaching are obviously big issues that relate to one of the core drivers of church life – Sunday gathered teaching and preaching. But the sacred-secular divide can penetrate something as small as a slide with the words of a hymn on it. Take a hymn like "Be Thou My Vision," which begins:

Be thou my vision, O Lord of my heart;
Naught be all else to me, save that thou art.

In many churches, the words of hymns and songs are projected onto the background of a sunset over the ocean or a beautiful countryside scene. There's nothing wrong with those pictures. The heavens do declare the glory of God, and many of us do feel closer to God out in his creation. However, such visuals imply that God is to be found in nature, in escape from our usual contexts, not *in* our everyday contexts.

You would almost never see the words of a hymn over a slum area in the local town, or over a factory, or over a picture of dishes in a sink, or a nightclub. But the pastor who puts pictures like those behind hymns has a much richer view of the scope of God's concern, of where God may be found and of what the role of God's people in the world might be, than the pastor who uses a picture of a golden sunset.

What are we training pastors to do? What understanding of their own role in relation to God's people shapes our teaching and our assessments?

Are we training them to create communities whose members are intentionally seeking to help one another grow in fruitfulness for Christ in all of life? On the whole, we are not. In fact, it is quite hard to find modules or courses in seminaries that are about helping other people grow as disciples in Christ. Indeed, while pastors expect to care for people with pastoral needs, they don't expect to help them work out how to make an impact for Christ in the factory they work in, never mind equip and train them to do so. That's the sacred-secular divide.

A while back, I (Mark) and my colleague Rev. Dr. Neil Hudson, a pioneer in creating whole-life disciple-making churches and the author of the ground-breaking *Imagine Church*,[6] met a young man called Ed at a conference. Ed was working in a factory and was overqualified for his job and bored by it. He'd prayed for a new job. Nothing happened. He'd asked his home group to pray that he'd get a new job. Nothing happened. He'd asked the church to pray that he'd get a new job. Nothing happened. I wonder what you might say to Ed?

In many parts of the world, you might simply point out that he is deeply blessed to be employed at all, and to be able to provide for himself and others through the work the Lord has given him.

You might respond pastorally: "Ed, the Lord is teaching you patience and perseverance. The Lord is sovereign and he will provide in his time."

You might respond practically: "Ed, maybe if you took the rings out of your nose and got a haircut you'd have more chance . . ."

Neil said, "Well, if you and your home group and your whole church have prayed and God hasn't given you a new job, then the question is: What does God want you to do there?" And he quoted Jeremiah 29:7: "Also, seek the peace and prosperity of the city to which I have carried you into exile. Pray to the LORD for it, because if it prospers, you too will prosper."

And Ed responded, "You mean I am meant to be a blessing there?"

So from then on, Ed got in ten minutes early for his shift and connected to the people going off shift and to the ones coming on shift. He began to pray for people without them knowing, and then to pray for people with them knowing it. Was his job still boring? Yes. Was his day boring? No. He was working with God.

This looks like a little thing, but it's a big thing both for Ed and for what it says about the scope of the pastor-people relationship. Church members expect to be cared for in crisis, but they often don't expect to be equipped for mission in their daily activities. And this represents a significant but necessary

---

6. Neil Hudson, *Imagine Church: Releasing Whole-Life Disciples* (Nottingham: Inter-Varsity Press, 2012).

shift for the self-understanding and role of ordained clergy: from pastoral care to whole-life disciple-making and equipping for mission; from running the activities of the local church to inspiring and enabling people to make an impact for Christ in their daily lives wherever they are.

What Neil did was to help Ed see how he could participate in the mission of God right where he was. And that is one of the things that church leaders are meant to do: give people a whole-life missional vision and disciple them to live it out.

We see this in Jesus's praxis. Yes, in his public ministry he spent a great deal of time teaching large groups of people, and indeed dealing with physical and spiritual disease, but he seems to have spent most time with a small group in an interactive, dialogical context – making disciples.

But it was not only in his own practice that Jesus focused on disciple-making; this disciple-making imperative was passed along to his followers. In Matthew's account Jesus's famous last words were: "Go . . . and make disciples of all nations, baptizing them in the name of the Father and of the Son and of the Holy Spirit, and teaching them to obey everything I have commanded you" (Matt 28:19–20).

He did not say "Go and make converts," but "Go and make disciples." There is a world of difference between a convert and a disciple. A convert has reached his or her destination; a disciple is on a journey of learning to live the way of Jesus in every area of life.

Indeed, when Jesus spoke those words, I suspect that those early disciples who had spent the last three years with him would have understood him to mean, "Go and have with others the kind of relationship that I've had with you."

And what kind of relationship was that? Interactive, ongoing, personal, eating, drinking, travelling, responding to questions, addressing issues of character and reflecting proactively with them on their experience. How many of us have ever had a relationship with an older Christian like that? How many of us have relationships with people in our congregations that look like that? How many seminaries have trained their students to have disciple-making relationships with anyone? In our global study we found very few examples of these types of relationships and training initiatives.

What the sacred-secular divide has done is not just shrink our understanding of the scope of disciple-making, but rather blind us to its necessity. Theological education exists to serve the church: not necessarily to provide what the sacred-secular divided church tells us it needs, but to provide what the church actually needs to serve the *missio Dei* in our context at this time in history.

The challenge of creating Monday to Sunday disciple-making missional communities will not be met merely by new resources, new programs or new training modules, but by a concerted effort to change the core culture of the local church into a whole-life missionary culture. The role of seminaries is to ensure that students have the theological grounding, the exegetical skills, the leadership will and the practical skills to do it.

As mentioned, the Langham Partnership and LICC have been involved in a two-year research project to help develop best practice. We set up four four-day collaborative workshops with theological educators from a range of institutions in Europe, Latin America, Africa and Asia. The aims were threefold:

- To learn how the sacred-secular divide manifests itself in different cultural contexts;
- To identify best practice – what works, why, what's transferable;
- To test and develop tools that generate awareness of the issues, and tools that combat the issues and create a new whole-life culture.

We learned much along the way. We were encouraged by examples of liberating practice in institutional culture, in curriculum design and in assessment. Indeed, there were more than enough examples of different interventions to convince us that anyone at any level in theological education can begin to make a difference in their own context – even if it may take longer to change an overall course or the institution as a whole. It doesn't need money or specialist training. Prayer, imagination, initiative and curiosity about the texture of people's everyday lives in the world are a heady combination.

The results of that work are published in *Whole-Life Mission for the Whole Church: Overcoming the Sacred-Secular Divide through Theological Education*,[7] with contributions from theological educators from around the world. The book casts a vision for whole-life discipleship and the whole-life disciple-making church. It looks at the sacred-secular divide in the light of Scripture, and then surveys key sources in historic and contemporary theological reflection. It

---

7. Greene and Shaw, *Whole-Life Mission*.

explores the principles that can fuel concrete changes to curriculum, modules, individual lectures, institutional culture and our own discipleship, offering examples of best practice from around the world. Our prayer is that, along with the work of this conference, it will contribute to an infectious, dynamic whole-life disciple-making culture that our students can carry into their ministries in church and society.

Questions for Personal Reflection and Group Discussion

1. Take a moment to reflect on the example shared at the beginning of the chapter of Victoria, who serves God and ministers to others through her work as a hairdresser. In your own context, do you know someone like Victoria who consciously fulfils his or her calling of Christian discipleship, service and mission through his or her daily vocational work?

2. If you have thought of an example of someone like Victoria, share it with the members of your discussion group. What formative influences have shaped (or continue to shape) this person's understanding of his/her work, calling, discipleship and mission?

3. As you reflect on the example of Victoria (and your own examples), how would you answer the following questions that the author poses:

- What kind of church community makes disciples like Victoria?
- What kind of church leader produces disciples like Victoria?
- What kind of seminary produces church leaders who produce disciples like Victoria?

4. Do the answers to question 3 reinforce your behaviour or create a need to change? Pray for wisdom to apply these ideas in your relationships and teaching.

5. If you teach in a seminary, reflect on ways in which the sacred-secular divide manifests itself in the institutional culture of the seminary, in curricular emphases and in your own teaching. Several examples may be shared and analysed constructively by the group.

6. Discuss ways in which the sacred-secular divide is evident in the evangelical churches of your context, considering aspects such as local church programs and

priorities, institutional culture, common assumptions regarding discipleship, ministry and mission, and so on.

7. What practical ideas can you suggest that could help seminaries and churches in your context become more effective in what the authors describe as "Monday to Saturday discipleship" and "whole-life disciple-making"?

8. Commit to praying for those in your group, that they might be able to implement such changes.

References

Cray, G. *Disciples and Citizens: A Vision for Distinctive Living.* Nottingham: Inter-Varsity Press, 2007.

———. *Who's Shaping You? 21st Century Disciples.* Harpenden: Cell UK, 2010.

Greene, Mark. "Is Anybody Listening?" *Anvil* 14, no. 4 (1997): 283–294.

———. *The One About . . . 8 Stories about God in Our Everyday Lives.* London: LICC, 2017.

Greene, Mark, and Ian Shaw, eds. *Whole-Life Mission for the Whole Church: Overcoming the Sacred-Secular Divide through Theological Education.* Carlisle: Langham Global Library, 2021.

Hudson, Neil. *Imagine Church: Releasing Whole-Life Disciples.* Nottingham: Inter-Varsity Press, 2012.

Sayers, D. L. "Why Work?" In *Letters to a Diminished Church: Passionate Arguments for the Relevance of Christian Doctrine.* Nashville: Thomas Nelson, 2004.

Section 4

A Call from across the Divide

In the previous sections, we have heard different "calls": to integration, for virtues, and to the church. In the present section, we hear a "Macedonian-like" call: those from the scholarly divide (academics in the university) are asking for help from theologians in how they can effectively fulfil their calling as Christian academics. There is a realization among a growing number of Christian academics of the need for a deeper understanding and more sophisticated knowledge of theology. Specialists in their own fields, these scholars need the kind of theological knowledge that matches their own expertise.

This section provides practical insights into how theologians and academics can work together in forming a hermeneutical community. It challenges scholars from the two sides of the divide to go beyond their own disciplines. For theologians, this would require imagining what theology would look like in the context of the university. What questions, issues and concerns do academics have that call for the theologians' contribution? One hindrance is the over-specialization and dichotomies among the disciplines. This is true especially in the seminary, where it is common to hear comments such as "The theologian never speaks with the biblical scholar," and vice versa. For theologians to even begin to think about how they can extend help to other scholars across the divide, they need to learn first how to collaborate with each other within the seminary.

The good news is that we now have models or attempts for how to do this. In this section, we are given some examples of how theologians and academics in other fields have worked together in ways that enabled each to contribute to the other. The hope is that theologians will see their calling not only in the seminary and the church but to the wider society.

8

Where Are the Theologians?
A Call from across the Scholarly Divide

Terence Halliday

I first express my thanks to Dr. Riad Kassis and the convenors of this consultation for inviting me, as an outsider to theological education, to join your rich conversations at this conference. It has been inspiring and uplifting. I have learnt a great deal.

I begin with a text we know very well:

> In the beginning was the Word, and the Word was with God, and the Word was God. He was with God in the beginning. *Through him all things were made; without him nothing was made that has been made.* In him was life, and that life was the light of all mankind. The light shines in the darkness, and the darkness has *not* overcome it. (John 1:1–5, emphasis added)

I am an academic sociologist who specializes in global legal change.[1] During some fieldwork in Hong Kong a few weeks before this conference I spoke to a bold and courageous Christian law professor at the University of Hong Kong who has taken a powerful stand against attacks on freedom of speech and freedom of assembly and for peaceful protest and democracy in

---

1. For further details see "Terence Halliday," American Bar Foundation, http://www. americanbarfoundation.org/faculty/profile/10.

Hong Kong. For this he has already paid a high price, including imprisonment. I asked him, "Where do you get your theological understanding to take the stand of public leadership you do?" He said (and I paraphrase), "I have a close Christian brother, a theologian, who sits with me and enables me to discern what the good society in Hong Kong should be and how to help build it."

Let me indulge in some shameless advertising which helps frame my perspective. Last year my co-author and I published our book *Global Lawmakers*[2] on how the United Nations makes laws to govern world trade. Our questions were simple to ask, though difficult to answer. Who makes laws for the world? Whose voices dominate and whose voices are silent? How do those laws influence global trade? Who benefits and who loses? How might global law-making be done differently to make it more legitimate, equitable, and so on?

Of course, I know fairly well how to think about these issues as a sociologist of law and markets – although reviewers may disagree! I believe I am equipped to influence in some small way global governance of commerce and trade. But I am also a person of faith. I am a citizen of the kingdom of God. Surely I am called *both* to advance knowledge and understanding in my scholarly field *and* to build the kingdom of God in my sphere of work.

My challenge is how to do both. I cross the world in my academic guise. As a faculty volunteer with the International Fellowship of Evangelical Students (IFES), I speak to groups of students and faculty on almost every continent. And everywhere I go, directly or indirectly, faculty and students raise the same question: *How* do I think Christianly? This makes me certain that this is not my problem alone.

There are hundreds and thousands of us, Christian professors who need to be equipped to think Christianly.

- We are in faculties of agriculture and departments of economics.
- We are in schools of fine arts and institutes of legal studies.
- We are in centres of disease control and faculties of arts.
- You can find us in business schools and literary studies.
- We are present in faculties of forestry and architecture.

---

2. Susan Block-Lieb and Terence C. Halliday, *Global Lawmakers: International Organizations in the Crafting of World Markets* (Cambridge/New York: Cambridge University Press, 2017).

- We are in public policy think tanks and schools of education.
- We work with nuclear accelerators and underwater drones.
- Wherever there is higher education, we are there.

And God has placed us there for the purposes of building his kingdom. But many of us, perhaps all of us, are incomplete. Yes, we might have advanced qualifications in our academic fields. Yes, we may have mastered our field. Yes, we may be at the leading edge of inquiry. Yes, we may be teachers of a rising generation or advisors to governments and international organizations.

But we suffer from a great weakness: most of us are theologically ill-equipped. There is an enormous asymmetry between the level of our scholarly understanding and the level of our theological sophistication. We might have doctoral qualifications in our scholarly field, but our theology remains at an elementary or secondary school level.

My challenge today therefore is quite simple – and quite bold. Where are the theologians? Where are our sisters and brothers in the faith who are strong where we are weak? Where are conversation partners, interlocutors, thinkers, who can lift us out of illiteracy, who can equip us to be fully rounded servants in the fertile terrain of the university? I call from across the scholarly divide for your help – help to enable us to address "all things" we study in the university through the eyes of faith.

Some Clarifications

Let me begin with some specifications.

First, for simplicity's sake I am going to use the term "seminary" to cover every kind of theological education represented at this consultation.

Second, I am going to use the term "theology" to mean any thoughtful understanding of God and his work "in all things."

Third, I use the term "theologian" quite loosely to refer to all faculty or teachers in seminaries, although I address a particular call to those who would describe themselves as theologians.

Fourth, I use the term "university" to refer to any institution of higher education and advanced research and scholarship.

Fifth, when I speak of "faculty," I include higher education teachers, postgraduate students, postdoctoral students, and researchers in institutes of advanced studies.

Why This Challenge Is Timely

One of the constants across the Scriptures is *surprise*. There are three happenings at this present moment which lead me to believe a new possibility for relationships is breaking open for theologians and scholars in the other disciplines.

First, I discern a small ferment, a stirring, a quickening of the Spirit, across the world among Christians in and near universities. At Oxford University this takes the form of a vibrant program for professors and graduate students on "developing a Christian mind."[3] The US InterVarsity movement's Graduate and Faculty Ministries urge students and faculty to "integrate faith and learning."[4] Within the last decade, I have participated in a growing worldwide movement within IFES to "engage the university."[5] The Yale University philosopher-theologian Nicholas Wolterstorff stimulated a book series on seeing academic disciplines "through the eyes of faith."

Second, in many parts of the world there is a capstone cohort of senior professors just retired, approaching retirement or imagining retirement. Many of these Christian professors may be seeking a new call, in which they can bring the fullness of their academic careers to developing Christian minds in their universities.

Third, I am hearing stronger signals of two developments, at least in major universities in the Global North. On the one hand, as an eminent scholar at Cambridge University told me recently, there is a sense in some leading universities that secular self-confidence is beginning to falter and stumble. On

---

3. See Developing a Christian Mind at Oxford, https://dcmoxford.org/.
4. "Graduate and Faculty Ministries," InterVarsity, https://gfm.intervarsity.org/.
5. "Engaging the University," IFES, https://ifesworld.org/en/university/; "Vision," Resources for Engaging the University, http://engage.universityresources.org/.

the other hand, we see openings for thoughtful engagements about religion, and the rightful place of religions, including Christianity, inside the walls of the university.

Together these developments suggest we are at a critical moment when theologians are called to reach across the divide to give Christian faculty new vision and new insight about developing a Christian mind in every part of the university.

Why Cross the Divide?

Why should seminaries and theologians cross the divide? I have asked this question in recent months of many scholars, theologians and theological educators. They say:

Crossing the Divide Is Vital for Academics in the Disciplines

Academics are a strategic audience for the seminary. Academics often are at the forefront of discovery, thought and debate. Academics frequently can be found shaping public opinion and advising policymakers, whether local, national or international. Academics shape the minds of the next generation of professionals and leaders. If these academics are Christian they have a compelling need to be equipped and served. They are a vital organ of the church in its local presence and of the church universal.

Crossing the Divide Is Necessary for Theologians

A notable theologian recently told me that theologians need to demonstrate beyond the seminary why a doctrine matters. What is at stake with theology and theological ethics?

Like all of us, I am told, theologians need to be refreshed, sometimes by the still waters, at other times amidst thunder. Seminary teachers can broaden their theological imaginations by reaching outside the seminary to discover what questions preoccupy scholars in the disciplines on the other side of the divide.

Crossing the Divide Is Necessary for Pastors Leading Congregations

If the main products of seminaries are pastors and Christian leaders, then pastors must be equipped to speak to those in their congregations who are in universities and from universities. These lay people sitting in the church pews may be leaders in business, in government, in the military, in civil society and in the volunteer sector of society. In every one of these spheres they confront difficult issues, hard decisions, questions about how they should behave and what they should say. Because the highly educated tend to shape societies, they must be a strategic priority for pastors and the seminaries that train them.

Crossing the Divide Is Also Vital for Seminaries as Institutions

If seminaries are to be relevant to their societies then seminary leaders tell me they must be able to show that the Bible, and the great theologies that knit it together, make seminaries and theologians moral and spiritual interpreters and guides for *every* institution. By so doing seminaries are able to cultivate deepening support because they can be seen to be relevant to all of life.

How Far Does Your Theology Reach?

May I ask, respectfully, how far does your theology reach? How far across the divide does it extend?

I know that many seminaries rightly equip staff workers on university campuses to enrich the devotional lives of Christian students and to call students to follow Jesus.

I know that seminaries frequently and rightly fortify their students with the armoury of apologetics.

Today, however, I speak of a theology that penetrates every corner of the university's life, practices and thought.

I speak of a theology that can guide faculty in our research agendas.

I speak of a theology that shapes how we do our teaching and scholarship – in our classrooms, labs, research groups, academic networks or mentoring.

I speak of a theology that gives all faculty a psalmist's vocabulary of praise, of responses to God's glory as we see it revealed in the discoveries of his handiwork.

I speak of a theology that brings a moral sensibility to all the ways we can imagine that our scholarship fosters human flourishing.

Can you "lead us into paths of righteousness" as we ponder whether our research and writing show the love of God to the world? Can you show us how to evaluate ways our work enables flourishing? Can you help us see how our scholarship might inspire the church, challenge the church, and forge rich partnerships with the church?

Theology for What?

What are the issues, the topics, on which we call for conversations and partnership across the divide?

1. One approach is to think about the *big issues* of our times and regions.

The following list shows the big issues confronted Christianly by the Intensive Summer Studies program held by the Union of Evangelical Students of India (UESI) in New Delhi:

- Ethnic conflict
- Climate change
- International relations between India and China
- The politics of oil
- Decolonization
- Poverty and deprivation
- Black markets

The following are *societal issues* that students and faculty wanted to engage with as Christians that emerged in our retreat in Lima, Peru, with AGEUP, the IFES national movement in Peru:

- Job creation and entrepreneurship
- Corruption
- Agricultural alternatives for cocoa farmers
- Alternative sources of energy
- Identity issues in indigenous communities

2. Another approach is for a theology that addresses *pastoral concerns*.

We can see this admirably served by biblical commentators in the Langham Bible commentaries.

In Langham's *Africa Bible Commentary* we see half- to one-page briefs on critical topics for Africans: debt, democracy, initiation rites, refugees, street children, tribalism, witchcraft, among many others. In Langham's *South Asia Bible Commentary* we see critical issues for South Asians: caste, gurus, karma and fatalism, resurrection and reincarnation, yoga and meditation, among many others.

There is great merit in all these approaches, and I affirm them strongly. Nevertheless, we must go further. Why?

3. I believe we need to penetrate into the *technical areas*, the highly specific topics known only to the specialists in the disciplines. It is often in these areas that the frontiers of discovery and knowledge are to be found, long before they enter the public sphere or the science sections of *El País*, *Le Monde*, *The Guardian* or the *New York Times*, long before they become documentaries on *Al Jazeera* and elsewhere.

4. And, of course, there are many pressing *cross-disciplinary areas*.

The following are topics from faculty at Boston universities, including Harvard and the Massachusetts Institute of Technology, at our retreat last year:

- Does international trade hurt the poor?
- Are randomized controlled trials the gold standard for public policymaking?
- How can we reach sustainability in energy, agriculture, healthcare, the environment?
- How can we take ethical approaches to discoveries in biotechnology?
- How can we use discourse and narrative to empower the oppressed?
- How do we understand types of security – food, economic, confidentiality, privacy, safety, crime?

Yet I believe we must go farther still. This we seek to do in a developing faculty initiative focused initially on research universities.[6]

I need theological support not of the relationship of sociology to faith in general, science in general, law in general or economics in general, though all are worthy topics.

I speak of what the astrophysicist is currently researching and publishing.

I speak of the current project the business law professor is designing.

I speak of what theory the development economist is currently refining.

Theology must penetrate to the frontier of knowledge in every faculty.

What Kind of Theology?

It is perfectly reasonable for you to ask: What kind of theology can possibly reach these problems? It is unreasonable to expect theological insight and gloss on every issue we work on. The list is endless, dynamic and enormously heterogeneous. Perhaps there is another way.

Donald Hay, Fellow of Jesus College and former Pro Vice Chancellor at Oxford University, and I, together with senior scholars in theology and the disciplines, are initiating a Faculty Initiative to build robust bridges across the divide. We are experimenting with approaches that are strong both in theology and in the disciplines. This approach imagines a design in two dimensions.

On one dimension of our effort – from my side of the divide – we aim to meet the needs of lecturers and professors across all the main faculties we observe in universities across the world. These include Agriculture, Architecture, Fine and Performing Arts, Humanities, Law, Medicine, Public Policy, Public Health, Engineering, Social Sciences, Biological and Physical Sciences.

On another dimension of our initiative – from your side of the divide – we envisage three or four clusters of topics that arise again and again to meet our work within universities.

---

6. Led by Donald Hay (Oxford University) and Terence Halliday (American Bar Foundation & Australian National University), the Faculty Initiative is "an initiative seeking to promote the integration of Christian faith and academic disciplines in research universities worldwide." https://facultyinitiative.net/.

1. Four Theologies: Creation, Fall, Redemption, Hope

At the Faculty and Graduate Student stream in the 2015 World Assembly of IFES, Dr. Vinoth Ramachandra, IFES Secretary for Dialogue and Social Engagement, urged academics to learn theologies of creation, reconciliation and revelation, among others.

In our Faculty Initiative we will begin with theologies that readily can be seen to reach across the faculties of the university, including creation, fall, redemption, hope.

2. Grand Themes

In graduate student and faculty workshops and retreats I find that several great biblical themes or motifs resonate widely. They can surprise professors who may never have been asked to imagine how these themes may have relevance to their academic work.

Among these themes are awe/wonder, beauty, creativity, flourishing, justice, love, order and wisdom. You will see immediately that several of these are perfectly acceptable topics across even the most secular or anti-religious of universities.

3. Virtues

Rather surprisingly, in God's providence, there is a growing interest, certainly in some universities with which I am familiar, with character and the virtues. The Oxford Pastorate[7] has a remarkable project, for instance, on character and the university, which provides openings for conversations in universities that directly connect with virtues we seek to cultivate in our faith.

What Kind of Engagement?

We intend to bridge the divide by opening up a two-way conversation.

---

7. Oxford Pastorate, https://oxfordpastorate.org/.

From the side of the seminary, we will invite theologians to write a "Theological Brief" (5,000–8,000 words) on each of these "theologies" in a way that is easily understood by scholars in all the disciplines.[8]

From the side of the disciplines, we will invite Christian scholars from each and any faculty within the university to write an even shorter brief – a "Disciplinary Brief" – of about 3,000–5,000 words in response from the vantage point of a particular project, interest or piece of writing they are currently engaged in.

In this way we hope that very good theology can encounter very good disciplinary scholarship, and each will be enriched by the other. Quality is assured on both sides.

Theology from Where?

In one sense, of course, our theology is universal.

In another sense, however, our understandings of God and his work, our readings of the Scriptures, are deeply contextual and we need to encounter cross-cultural theology.

We need local theologians (with their theological understandings) who attend to the challenges of the local, national and regional. And those of us in one region – North America, for instance – desperately need the regenerative insights of theology coming from other regions.

The theological "commons" we must create, therefore, is a meeting place for all the faculties of the university to meet theologies from all corners of the church universal, wherever theology and scholarship is found.

Let us get more practical.

Incomplete Solutions

There are several ways in which this challenge of crossing the divide has been approached. Each has merits, but each also has limits.

---

8. As of late 2020 four theologians have committed to write "Theology Briefs": Nicholas Wolterstorff (Yale University) on justice; Nigel Biggar (Oxford University) on created order; Miroslav Volf (Yale University) on flourishing; and Alister McGrath (Oxford University) on a topic to be decided.

One is for the disciplinary scholar to know her or his Bible. Of course, this is critical, yet it is not enough. Thanks to godly parents, I have been immersed in the Scriptures from my youth. But I found that this does *not* equip me to think theologically – to think with the breadth, the depth and the incisiveness that is required to permeate adequately my academic work with the richness of meanings of our faith.

Another is for a scholar in the disciplines who is also a Christian to write a book where he or she provides his or her own theology. The danger is that this scholar's theology does not reach the same level of quality as her or his regular scholarship.

A third approach goes in the opposite direction. A theologian looks across the divide, chooses a topic, and writes theological reflections on a discipline or big issue. Here the level of theological reflection may be high. The danger is that a theologian might appear naïve to scholar specialists in a field.

A fourth approach is to ask disciplinary scholars to become theologians themselves. Very occasionally this happens with rare individuals such as Professor Alister McGrath at Oxford, who serves on our convening panel, or Dr. Leigh Trevaskis, Principal of Trinity College, Queensland, who obtained double doctorates, one in a discipline, one in theology. But that is far beyond most of us.

Can We Imagine Practical Solutions?

Here I offer some ways forward. Some have been tried; others have been suggested to me, mostly by seminary leaders and theologians.

1. *Disciplinary scholars find a theological partner.* My colleague at the Australian National University, international relations scholar Dr. Luke Glanville, is writing a book jointly with his brother, a pastor/ theologian from Canada. I have such a partnership with my colleague Professor K. K. Yeo at Garrett Evangelical Seminary and Northwestern University. These are ideal situations but rare.

2. In some very fortunate circumstances there may be *clusters of Christian disciplinary scholars* and theologically trained people in a local congregation or community. For many years I met every Friday

morning for an hour and a half with a band of fellow Christians at my home church, FPCE. They all were ordained pastors and three were widely published theologians. They provoked me to talk about my research and writing. In turn, they gave it theological meaning and pointed me in constructive directions, widening my horizons.

3. *Invite disciplinary scholars to the seminary to give a talk* – in plain language – about their work. These would be persons from different disciplines – e.g. from aesthetics or biological sciences – to have them present and thus spark theological engagement. From here closer ongoing relationships might emerge.

4. *Adopt a university*, discover Christian faculty in the university, and draw them into dialogue and conversation. Many cities in various parts of the world have sister cities. My home city of Evanston, in the Chicago area, has a sister city in Belize. Could seminaries forge relationships with sister universities, even if informally?

5. Within seminaries create *a workshop*, even a course or seminar, where students are taught great theological themes, and where academics from other disciplines can bring their "problems." This would be a way of exercising the muscles of the mind on both sides: bringing disciplinary scholars towards theology, and activating theological engagement with the disciplines.

6. In some seminaries there are *public theology* courses. They can go some way towards being more explicit about wider generic issues that play out in various spheres of life, including the academic life.

7. Groups of disciplinary scholars may form *scholarly circles in which they invite theologians as commentators*. We created such a circle of doctoral students and faculty in *international relations* at the Australian National University. Each of the international studies specialists wrote draft papers, and we invited theologians from nearby St Marks National Theological Centre to comment on our papers and join wider conversations. We are now preparing these for submission to a journal of public theology.

8. And then there are more remote ways, using the *Internet and social media*, where theologians can inspire and the disciplinary scholars can respond, as we are planning in our Faculty Initiative.

What Kind of Theologian Do We Need?

Here is another practicality I have been pondering: What kind of person do we long for to help us bridge the scholarly divide?

Surely there are personal qualities. Someone who

- Is interested
- Feels my passion
- Listens
- Is thoughtful
- Makes time
- Takes risks

There are also theological qualities. This person will need

- A theological sensibility – can think beyond the text;
- A theological imagination – can bring theology to places it may not have been before;
- An understanding of theological traditions – can draw on the rich tradition of the faith;
- An ability to translate theologies into accessible language – can converse easily with non-theologians.

Realism: Barriers and Objections

If we are to be practical, we must also be realistic. We confront many barriers and numbers of objections to pursuing this vision.

Let me begin from the disciplines side. I do not for a moment want to convey the message that this divide between the disciplines and the seminaries is entirely the making of seminaries. That would be quite wrong.

We, on the disciplinary side, are a great part of the problem. Many of us, even a majority of Christian faculty, do not recognize that we are called to think Christianly about our scholarship.

Many of us hide in our offices unwilling to open ourselves up to new theological vistas. Life is hard enough on our side of the divide without crossing over to your side.

We are afraid of theology. We think it is another language, another way of thinking, another epistemology that is beyond us.

From the seminary side, I have asked seminary leaders and theologians what difficulties they confront, even if they enthusiastically support this vision of bridging the divide. They say:

- Seminaries are remote from universities.
- Seminary faculty lack strong disciplinary backgrounds.
- The theological guild is too specialized or has a limited view of theology's province.
- Theologians focus on being technically correct and are afraid to drift too far from the text.
- Seminaries are already under-resourced.
- Faculty feel over-worked.
- Seminaries lack confidence in what they can contribute to university worlds. As Nicholas Wolterstorff[9] has said, they've come to believe that the flow of influence comes from the disciplines to theology, not from theology to the disciplines.
- An underlying ecclesiology assumes serving the church writ narrowly is what matters.

Looking Forward

For too long, too many of us have lived in different worlds: a disciplinary world with shallow theological depth; or a faith world with confined theological borders. A divide has separated us.

Yet the Spirit is moving – in the university world, in seminaries, amongst scholars of all kinds, in all regions of the world. We have a wonderful possibility of creating bridges across the divide, of joining hands, and of expanding hearts and minds.

We began with John 1. I conclude with Colossians 1:

In him [Christ] all things were created: things in heaven and on earth, visible and invisible, whether thrones or powers or rulers or authorities; all things have been created through him and for

---

9. Nicholas Wolterstorff, *Religion in the University* (New Haven: Yale University Press, 2019).

him. He is before all things, and in him all things hold together. (Col 1:16–17)

My plea is that you, theological educators, will step across the divide. Invite us to join you in dialogue, so together we may demonstrate to ourselves and our worlds that "in him *all* things hold together."

Questions for Personal Reflection and Group Discussion

1. What answers would you give to the question posed to the author by students and faculty: "How do I think Christianly?" Share the perspectives you consider most important.

2. Reflect on the relation between theological and higher education in your own local and national context and discuss to what degree the divide that Halliday describes exists. Share examples of any initiatives you are aware of that serve to help theologians and academics to "cross the divide."

3. Imagine that Dr. Halliday has just delivered a presentation of this chapter to the faculty of your theological institution and ended with this invitation:

> My challenge today therefore is quite simple – and quite bold. Where are the theologians? Where are our sisters and brothers in the faith who are strong where we are weak? Where are conversation partners, interlocutors, thinkers, who can lift us out of illiteracy, who can equip us to be fully rounded servants in the fertile terrain of the university? I call from across the scholarly divide for your help – help to enable us to address "all things" we study in the university through the eyes of faith.

(a) What sort of barriers do you envisage to the response to this invitation? How might these barriers be overcome?

(b) Discuss practical ways your faculty might respond to this challenge in dialogue with Christian teachers, university professors and academics from your context.

4. As you reflect upon the teaching focus of your faculty members, propose and discuss examples of cross-disciplinary questions that might be fruitfully explored by Christian theologians and academics.

5. What benefits might these interdisciplinary studies and reflections have for the church, society and theological institutions in your context?

6. What practical steps could be taken to facilitate such dialogue between individual theologians and academics? Between your institution and other institutions or groups of academics?

7. Pause and pray for yourself, your colleagues and your Christian brothers and sisters who fulfil their callings "across the divide" as teachers, university professors and academics.

References

Wolterstorff, Nicholas. *Religion in the University*. New Haven: Yale University Press, 2019.

Websites

Developing a Christian Mind at Oxford. https://dcmoxford.org/.
"Engaging the University." IFES. https://ifesworld.org/en/university/.
Faculty Initiative. https://facultyinitiative.net/.
"Graduate and Faculty Ministries." InterVarsity. https://gfm.intervarsity.org/.
Oxford Pastorate. https://oxfordpastorate.org/.
"Terence Halliday." American Bar Foundation. http://www.americanbarfoundation.org/faculty/profile/10.
"Vision." Resources for Engaging the University. http://engage.universityresources.org/.

Postscript

ICETE 2018 and Then COVID-19

Reflections and Prayers on the Sacred-Secular Divide and Our COVID-19 Contexts

A New Context for Reflection on the Sacred-Secular Divide

In early 2018, the looming pandemic was not on the minds of those invited to give plenary addresses and workshops at the ICETE triennial consultation, as they wrote and reflected upon the significant challenges and missional opportunities that the so-called sacred-secular divide poses for the global church and for evangelical theological institutions.

Neither was the pandemic on the minds of the hundreds of attendees from across the globe who gathered in Panama for five days in September 2018. The challenges and opportunities to be presented by the pandemic were not addressed by the speakers nor unpacked in the workshops, and they formed no part of the reflection and personal application of the participants. At that time, the new normal of 2020 was unforeseeable and unthinkable, and the most we could do was explore the challenges of bridging the sacred-secular divide in relation to the normal of our local contexts as we knew it in late 2018.

Even as 2019 turned to 2020, very few beyond the spheres of government and public health could have predicted the tremendous implications (health, social, financial, educational, technological, religious, political and more) of the virus that would rapidly spread across countries and regions in the early months of the new year.

For theological institutions, educators and students, teaching and learning began in 2020 in the usual way, and few could have imagined the changes that would soon sweep across the whole world: the closure of public spaces and the prohibition of public gatherings, working from home, shelter-in-place orders and travel restrictions. Quarantines and curfews, face masks, alcohol gel and social distancing soon became a part of daily life. Within a space of weeks, seminary campuses were closed, students were sent home, and administrators, faculty and students made the abrupt transition to emergency remote teaching or to online education. Beyond the formidable logistical and educational implications of the pandemic, many schools struggled to stay afloat under the weight of enormous financial burdens. Churches faced similar challenges, conditions and restrictions. As the pandemic spread across our communities and made public meetings dangerous, Christian leaders were forced to discover and invent new ways to continue to do the very things that the church is called to do in every age and every circumstance. In the context of a new normal that felt very strange, church leaders and committed disciples found new ways to minister, virtually and through distancing strategies, and new ways to participate in God's mission to their hurting communities amidst the great hardships and new conditions presented by the pandemic.

COVID-19 was not a localized phenomenon that only happened to others in distant places. It happened to all of us everywhere. The constant barrage of bad news disseminated through social networks and the media has been distressing and disheartening, and has wearied us over time. The pandemic has left none of us unchanged and no community unscathed. Some who read this postscript will have lost loved ones: family, friends and ministry colleagues. Perhaps they will have been sick themselves.

Those who serve in theological institutions and churches will be painfully aware of the way in which the pandemic has ravaged the lives of members of their educational and faith communities, as well as the communities in which we live. In these challenging times, new stresses have been added to existing ones. Many have felt understandably overwhelmed in the struggle to adapt and keep pace with rapid changes, and to meet the multiple commitments of daily life in the family, church, seminary and community.

Doing Theology in a New Context

As God's people cry out to the Lord in the midst of struggle, sickness, death and mourning, and continue to cry out in the wake of all that the pandemic brought and has left behind, the biblical language of lament is particularly appropriate. Of course, as in many of the lament psalms, even in deep personal and national crises God's faithful ones turn from lament to praise and petition.

In this postscript we want to give brief indications of some theological concepts which bring together the sacred-secular divide and the experience of COVID-19. We also want to provide a pattern for prayer around the major themes of this book.

Writers and editors do not live within the pages of their books. Neither do readers. Those who wrote, those who edited and those who will read this work all live in the real world. We must now reinterpret and apply the guidance given within the contexts in which we live, drastically altered and removed from the contexts in which this guidance was originally given and received in 2018.

This is a hermeneutical task that we are accustomed to, in the interpretation and application of the message of the Scriptures to our own lives and to the lives of those we serve in our educational, faith and local communities. A similar task of contextualization will be necessary for the reader to apply the perspectives of this book to the challenges and opportunities of the sacred-secular divide in a COVID- and post-COVID world.

It is in the light of these new realities that the authors' four calls must now be interpreted and applied: the call to integration, the call for virtue, the call to the church, and the call to seminaries from across the sacred-secular divide.

A Call to Integration

It is in this context that we must interpret Wright's encouragement to draw consolation, hope and renewed strength as we reflect upon the unchangeable fact of God's uniqueness, past record and future mission. In situations in which we feel harried and hurried, and drawn in many directions, we are encouraged to call upon the Lord to unite our hearts once again to fear his name and to serve with integrity (Ps 86:11).

It is also in the context of the new normal that we must wrestle with Ho's proposal to apply the insights of a more biblical worldview, abandoning the traditional sacred-secular dichotomy in favour of a sacred and more sacred continuum that recognizes that all God's universe is in some degree sacred, by virtue of his creative work, his presence and his original and redemptive purposes that act in it. This new way of contemplating God's world and discerning his work will help change the way we see everything and everyone, and help transform daily life (previously relegated to the plane of the secular or mundane) and our interactions with others (created in God's image) into a missional quest to see God's name glorified, his purposes fulfilled and all aspects of life increasingly sanctified.

In Psalm 86, the thanksgiving is followed by lament. After the psalmist expressed his thanksgiving (vv. 12–13), he again cries out to God, for "arrogant foes are attacking me" (v. 14). It is this movement from thanksgiving to lament that characterizes the experience of many of our institutions with the sudden and unexpected coming of the pandemic. We need to learn to live in this tragic change while believing that even the tragic has a place in the presence of God. Thanksgiving and lament can exist together because we have a God to whom we can cry out in the midst of our suffering. Like the psalmist, we can pray: "Turn to me and have mercy on me; show your strength on behalf of your servant" (v. 16).

Prayer

O LORD of mercy, we thank you that you are God not only in our joys and victories, but also in our sorrows and defeats. As we face our world today, grant us an undivided heart so that, like the psalmist, we will learn not only to bless you with all that is within us (Ps 103), but also to pour out our laments to you (Ps 102). Amen.

A Call for Virtue

It is within the context of the realities presented in the pandemic that we are invited to consider and apply the proposals of Chua, Oxenham and Naidoo with regards to the scope, means and ends of theological education. Building on Ho's chapter, Chua encourages us to apply the sacred and more sacred worldview to our vision of spiritual formation of students and to the type of ministry, cultural engagement and mission for which they are being prepared.

For his part, Oxenham urges the importance of character and virtue education as key to the holistic development of Christian leaders and as a way to impact society by sharing ideas, connecting with a felt need, and by living out the ethical and moral implications of the gospel.

A virus that knows no geographical, political, social, cultural or religious boundaries has caused us to realize that, for better or worse, we are all much more connected than we imagined. In the light of the pandemic, the Christian imperative to love our neighbour is expressed or negated by an action as simple as wearing a mask. Seemingly abstruse ethical considerations, such as the case for solidarity over egocentrism, are shown to have real-world consequences. Along these same lines, readers will be challenged by Naidoo to consider identity formation as a vital aspect of training for ministry, and to rethink the Christian disciple and servant's self-understanding and role in society against the backdrop of the needs and opportunities created by the coronavirus.

The pandemic has brought about a renewed focus on the church's engagement with society. One of the things the pandemic has done is to expose the weaknesses of government in some countries. There are cases where, instead of focusing on addressing the COVID-19 problem, some leaders have used the crisis to advance their own selfish interests. This is the case, for example, in the Philippines, where the government prioritized the passing of the Anti-Terror law – a law which many Filipinos see will terrorize ordinary people – instead of focusing on how to address the health crisis. The pandemic has done the same thing with some of our theological institutions. We are now beginning to realize how unprepared some churches and theological institutions are in responding to the crisis transpiring before our very eyes. One seminary president admits that we are at a loss as to how to respond to what is happening in our own context. The pandemic has also exposed the church's, as well as theological institutions', capacity or lack thereof to engage with society. This brings the topic of this book, the sacred-secular divide, to a new level of urgency.

Prayer

Gracious Father, you search our hearts and know us deep within. May we understand Spirit-given virtue which grows like fruit on a good tree. Help us to bear patiently, embrace your peace and show goodness, no matter what our circumstances. Help our institutions as they engage in society at this time, as

both servants and faithful saints confident of Christ's ultimate victory. Refine us
personally, in our ministries and in our seminaries. Amen.

A Call to the Church

Against this same backdrop, readers will be challenged by Reju and Tink, and
Greene and Shaw to rethink the roles of the church and theological institutions
in developing strategic initiatives that serve to equip, empower and commission
disciples to fulfil their diverse callings and vocation as Christians within their
daily occupations and professional lives. Biblically grounded perspectives of
the theology of work and a focus on whole-life discipleship are of particular
importance to churches and theological institutions as they work together to
prepare men and women for workplace ministry and mission. This vital task
will require much vision and creativity at a time when many disciples are
working from home or within the regimented constraints of social distancing,
or have been forced to change jobs or find new ways of providing for their
families in the midst of emergency conditions.

An important addition to creativity is discernment. What is God trying to
tell his church today? As the psalmist declares, "Today, if you hear his voice,
do not harden your hearts" (Ps 95:7–8 ESV). Psalm 95 contains some of the
most beautiful words for worship: "Oh come, let us sing to the LORD; let us
make a joyful noise to the rock of our salvation!" (v. 1 ESV). It also articulates
some of the most profound theologies, declaring God to be the "great King
who is above all gods" (v. 3), the creator God (v. 5) and the great Shepherd of
his people (v. 7). Yet in spite of all these truths, God had to warn his people,
lest they suffer the same judgment their forefathers experienced (vv. 9–11).
May God give us a discerning heart to hear what he is saying!

Prayer

Lord of wisdom, we humbly acknowledge our inability to comprehend your ways.
We do not know what your purpose is in bringing the pandemic to our world.
We do not understand how so much suffering and pain can suddenly overtake
us. We feel overwhelmed. Please help us! But more than this, teach us to hear,
to discern what your Spirit is telling us today. Through Christ our Lord, Amen.

A Call from across the Divide

Finally, Halliday's call and invitation to theological educators from across the academic divide is a timely one that deserves to be heeded in the extraordinary times and circumstances in which we find ourselves. There is much work to be done, and there are strategic opportunities to impact culture and orient the church as societies, around the world and at every level, search for answers to questions made urgent by the pandemic, questions that interdisciplinary teams of Christian theologians and academics are uniquely equipped to address.

The pandemic makes the call for interdisciplinary activity acutely important. We need all the resources we can muster to address our situation. The experts in the seminary must partner with those in the universities or secular institutions in framing responses to the many crises confronting us. Gone are the days when the biblical scholar can simply say, "My concern is only with what the text meant." For why was the Bible written? Is it not for the training for good works, which include the creation of jobs and promotion of health? Some of the disciplines in the secular universities are good with the questions "What?" and "How?" Theology and the Christion worldview is needed to provide answers to the "Why?"

Prayer

"Why, LORD, do you stand far off? Why do you hide yourself in times of trouble?" (Ps 10:1). There are so many things we do not understand. Some of us are asking: Why does it have to be the good people who suffer? Why not the wicked people? Our hearts go out for the least and the poor among us. How can they survive this pandemic? Lord, use us! Strengthen us and empower us! Teach us to work together for the sake of the weak and vulnerable. More than ever, the church and the theological institutions need your grace to continue their calling. Grant us creativity and discernment to move where your Spirit is leading us. We acknowledge that apart from your help, we will not be able to do anything. You are our hope. "You, LORD, hear the desire of the afflicted; you encourage them, and you listen to their cry" (Ps 10:17). Through Christ our Lord, we pray. Amen.

ICETE

Global Hub for Evangelical Theological Education

ICETE is a global community, sponsored by nine regional networks of theological schools, to enable international interaction and collaboration among all those engaged in strengthening and developing evangelical theological education and Christian leadership development worldwide.

The purpose of ICETE is:

1. To promote the enhancement of evangelical theological education worldwide.
2. To serve as a forum for interaction, partnership and collaboration among those involved in evangelical theological education and leadership development, for mutual assistance, stimulation and enrichment.
3. To provide networking and support services for regional associations of evangelical theological schools worldwide.
4. To facilitate among these bodies the advancement of their services to evangelical theological education within their regions.

Sponsoring associations include:

Africa: Association for Christian Theological Education in Africa (ACTEA)

Asia: Asia Theological Association (ATA)

Caribbean: Caribbean Evangelical Theological Association (CETA)

Europe: European Evangelical Accrediting Association (EEAA)

Euro-Asia: Euro-Asian Accrediting Association (E-AAA)

Latin America: Association for Evangelical Theological Education in Latin America (AETAL)

Middle East and North Africa: Middle East Association for Theological Education (MEATE)

North America: Association for Biblical Higher Education (ABHE)

South Pacific: South Pacific Association of Evangelical Colleges (SPAEC)

www.icete-edu.org

☘ Langham
PARTNERSHIP

Langham Literature and its imprints are a ministry of Langham Partnership.

Langham Partnership is a global fellowship working in pursuit of the vision God entrusted to its founder John Stott –

> *to facilitate the growth of the church in maturity and Christ-likeness through raising the standards of biblical preaching and teaching.*

Our vision is to see churches in the Majority World equipped for mission and growing to maturity in Christ through the ministry of pastors and leaders who believe, teach and live by the word of God.

Our mission is to strengthen the ministry of the word of God through:
- nurturing national movements for biblical preaching
- fostering the creation and distribution of evangelical literature
- enhancing evangelical theological education

especially in countries where churches are under-resourced.

Our ministry

Langham Preaching partners with national leaders to nurture indigenous biblical preaching movements for pastors and lay preachers all around the world. With the support of a team of trainers from many countries, a multi-level programme of seminars provides practical training, and is followed by a programme for training local facilitators. Local preachers' groups and national and regional networks ensure continuity and ongoing development, seeking to build vigorous movements committed to Bible exposition.

Langham Literature provides Majority World preachers, scholars and seminary libraries with evangelical books and electronic resources through publishing and distribution, grants and discounts. The programme also fosters the creation of indigenous evangelical books in many languages, through writer's grants, strengthening local evangelical publishing houses, and investment in major regional literature projects, such as one volume Bible commentaries like *The Africa Bible Commentary* and *The South Asia Bible Commentary.*

Langham Scholars provides financial support for evangelical doctoral students from the Majority World so that, when they return home, they may train pastors and other Christian leaders with sound, biblical and theological teaching. This programme equips those who equip others. Langham Scholars also works in partnership with Majority World seminaries in strengthening evangelical theological education. A growing number of Langham Scholars study in high quality doctoral programmes in the Majority World itself. As well as teaching the next generation of pastors, graduated Langham Scholars exercise significant influence through their writing and leadership.

To learn more about Langham Partnership and the work we do visit **langham.org**

www.ingramcontent.com/pod-product-compliance
Lightning Source LLC
Chambersburg PA
CBHW070041100426
42740CB00013B/2747